Access to the Past

DATE DUE

Access to the Past

Museum Programs and

Handicapped Visitors

A guide to Section 504—
making existing programs and
facilities accessible to
disabled persons

Alice P. Kenney

Drawings by Charles Cox

American Association for State and Local History

Nashville, Tennessee

Author and publisher make grateful acknowledgement to the Lehigh County (Pennsylvania) Historical Society and the National Endowment for the Humanities for permission to use in this book copyrighted material from *Hospitable Heritage: The Report of Museum Access* (Allentown, Pa.: Lehigh County Historical Society, 1979).

Library of Congress Cataloguing-in-Publication Data

Kenney, Alice P   1937–
   Access to the past.

   Bibliography: p.
   Includes index.
   1. Museums and the handicapped.   I. American Association
for State and Local History.   II. Title.
AM160.K46   069.1'7   80–24106
ISBN 0–910050–45–7

Research for and publication of this book was made possible by support from the National Endowment for the Arts.

Contents

Preface   vii

1   "Only Worried a Lot"   1
  "How Do You Define Disability?"   4
  "I Don't Know What Section 504 Is"   7
  "We Hadn't Really Thought Much about It"   11

2   "Things We Can Do Right Now"   21
  "A Board of Directors that Supports Such Efforts"   24
  "Many Things We Do Are Just Common Sense"   27
  "I Need Some Feedback"   37

3   "We Don't Have Any Special Programs"   45
  "We Are Doing Our Utmost to Have as Few Inaccessible
    Areas as Possible"   48
  "We Are Working to Increase the Scope of Our Communication"   58
  "The Basic Premise Is 'Don't Hover'"   67

4   "Good Ethics, Good Public Relations, Good Business"   81
  "Guided According to Their Capacity"   84
  "We Might Be Able to Develop a Program ... If We Could
    Generate Financial Support"   89
  "This Is Their World, Too"   95

Appendixes   103
  Appendix A: The Law   105
  Appendix B: Tabulations of Survey Responses   107
  Appendix C. Representative Programs at
    Historical Organizations   114
For Further Reading   122
Index   127

Preface

The American Association for State and Local History has been aware for some time of the anxiety among small museums and historical organizations concerning their responsibility for making their programs available to disabled persons. Although that became a legal as well as a moral obligation with the passage of the Rehabilitation Act of 1973, its practical implications were not spelled out until the issuance of guidelines for compliance with Section 504 of that act by various federal agencies, including the National Endowment for the Arts in 1979. Since these guidelines require that recipients of federal funds make their programs accessible to handicapped persons within three years, the question of how best to do so has become urgent. Many small museums and historical organizations are concerned about accomplishing structural modifications within the limits of their resources and program adaptations within the time their staff can spare from many other duties. They are also confused by conflicts between the requirement to provide access for disabled persons and that of preserving the integrity of historic structures laid down by the Historic Preservation Act of 1966. Nevertheless, some organizations have been tackling the problem and have accumulated experience that may be helpful to others.

The author of this book is a historian and educator who has developed a special interest in improving the accessibility of historic sites through a number of years of doing research in museums from a wheelchair. Interest generated by her articles on this subject prompted the Lehigh County (Pennsylvania) Historical Society to sponsor her proposal for a survey of museum accessibility to disabled persons in sixteen counties of southeastern Pennsylvania. Funded by the National Endowment for the Humanities, a federal agency, between 1977 and 1979, Museum Access studied facilities and programs at eighty-five museums, more than half of them in historic buildings. Its final report, *Hospitable Heritage,* was distributed to participants and to many others outside the project area who requested it. Since requests for it have outrun the supply, the most important of its contents have been incorporated in the present volume. Permission to use these copyrighted materials from the Lehigh County Historical Society and the National Endowment for the Humanities is greatly appreciated.

In planning this book, it became clear that the experience of a single region with a distinctive cultural tradition might not be fully applicable to the circumstances of historical organizations elsewhere. A survey questionnaire was therefore mailed to 750 member organizations of the American Association for State and Local History. Some of the considerable proportion who replied reported very interesting accommodations for disabled visitors, while others indicated the aspects of the subject on which they most needed information. Further correspondence with a number of them contributed many valuable insights, which, it is hoped, will be helpful to others. The author wishes to take this opportunity to thank everyone who responded for their time and trouble.

It is hoped that this book will be useful not only to staff members of small museums and historical organizations, but to the board members and volunteers who contribute so much to their programs. It may assist them in completing the "self-evaluation" required by the Section 504 guidelines and to discover many adjustments that can be put into practice with very little effort. It will also give them some basis for consultation with disabled individuals and groups and for training staff and volunteers to meet their needs. When these adaptations have been accomplished, it may suggest ways of making the unavoidable structural modifications within the limits of the organization's resources. In the process some administrators may well find, as have their counterparts in many other museums and historical organizations, that accommodations designed to benefit disabled persons increase the organization's effectiveness in interpreting the historic heritage of the community to their entire audience.

This book could not have been written without the help of

many people, only some of whom can be named here. Of the staff of Museum Access, Christine Fiedler assembled the bibliography, and Katherine Kidd edited the manuscript of *Hospitable Heritage*. The presidents and board of directors of the Lehigh County Historical Society contributed unfailing support, while Executive Directors Mahlon G. Hellerich, Allen F. Maybee, and Carol Wickkiser and their office staff gave much time-consuming assistance. Cedar Crest College provided office space, telephone and mailing privileges, and many other support services.

Museum staff members and other individuals have contributed many valuable insights. Raymond Shepherd reported on the National Trust for Historic Preservation pilot project for improving accessibility at Cliveden, in Philadelphia. Laura Rufe of the Bucks County (Pennsylvania) Historical Society and Tracy A. Van Rupper of Lyndhurst, New York, described interesting tours by groups of blind visitors. George Sheets of the York County (Pennsylvania) Historical Society explained their pioneer sign-language tours for the deaf, while Albert Pimintel of Gallaudet College (Washington, D.C.) and Diane Wilverdiz of the Margaret Sterck School for the Hearing-Impaired (Delaware) provided additional information. Linda Dean and Barbara Green discussed problems of learning-disabled children, and Beverly Tisdale related experiences of her mentally retarded son. Letitia Galbraith reported a Christmas party for retarded children at Shadows-on-the-Teche (Louisiana).

Special thanks are due to the persons who contributed the statements in Appendix C, which are printed with their permission. They are Bryn Evans of the Paul Revere Memorial Association (Massachusetts), Carl Hugh Jones of the Nebraska State Historical Society, and Carola G. Rupert and Allen Martin of the Macon County (Illinois) Historical Society. Others include Allen F. Maybee for the Lehigh County Historical Society, Shirley Willard of the Fulton County (Indiana) Historical Society, Liz Johnson of the Rocky Mount (Tennessee) Historical Society, and Joanna Wos of the Oswego County (New York) Historical Society. In addition, Shirley Cantino and Hans Joachim Finke reported activities of regional consortia. Katherine Kidd, Larry Molloy, and Joel Rodney made perceptive comments on the first draft.

The generous financial and moral support of national organizations is most gratefully acknowledged. That of the National Endowment for the Humanities for Museum Access provided an indispensable foundation for further research. The National Endowment for the Arts is sponsoring the present publication. The staff of the American Association for State and Local History have rendered thoughtful editorial supervision. Of course, none of these contributors is in any way responsible for the findings and conclusions of this work, which are entirely those of the author, except for the statements in Appendix C. These findings and conclusions do not necessarily represent the views of the National Endowment for the Arts, the National Endowment for the Humanities, or the American Association for State and Local History.

1

"Only Worried a Lot"

"BUILDINGS are preserved for people," concluded a statement of the National Trust for Historic Preservation on reconciling access for handicapped persons with the integrity of historic structures. This issue has become urgent as disabled people increasingly assert their right to participate in the full range of experiences that Americans in general take for granted. Disabled people have called attention to a wide range of barriers—architectural, communicational and attitudinal —that exclude them from many community activities. This exclusion has been far more often inadvertent than intentional, but many handicapped individuals regard it as discrimination. They have formed an active civil rights movement that has prompted federal, state, and local legislation, most notably Section 504 of the Rehabilitation Act of 1973. At the time of the bicentennial, they emphasized their eagerness to share on equal terms in the historic heritage of all Americans.

Historical organizations and museums of all kinds recognize their legal and moral obligation to meet that need, but many of them are bewildered as to how best to go about it. Small societies straining their resources to preserve a local landmark fear that they may be compelled to damage its historic character and overtax their budgets by installing a ramp or an elevator. Conscientious directors are overwhelmed by literature written primarily by and for large museums with numerous professional staff, highly developed programs, and extensive financial resources. Much of that literature, furthermore, is directed toward art museums concentrating on conserving priceless treasures, rather than toward smaller art museums or history museums focusing on preserving the character of a part of the past. Directors of many historical organizations would agree with the one whose response to a survey question on Section 504 compliance was: "Only worried a lot." This book has been prepared in the hope that it will help administrators and staffs of museums and historical organizations to stop worrying and start acting constructively.

3

"How Do You Define Disability?"

The historical society director who asked "How do you define disability?" shares that perplexity with many fellow citizens, because there is no consensus on what constitutes a disability. Estimates of the number of handicapped persons in the United States vary greatly, but it is clear that there are far more of them than has sometimes been supposed. The general federal census has not, in the past, collected information on this subject, but the 1980 census long form does include a question on whether disability interferes with any person's employment or use of public transportation. Though some state agencies compile statistical data on the people they serve, others do not. A widely used figure is 35 million, or one in six Americans, though other calculations run as high as 51 million, or one in four. These figures include roughly equal proportions of persons with limited mobility, vision, hearing, and mental capacity, an appreciable number of whom have multiple disabilities. Alcoholism and drug abuse have also been defined as handicaps by recent federal court decisions.

Persons with limited mobility may include 11.7 million permanently disabled, as well as another 12.5 million temporarily incapacitated by injuries. People with limited mobility may use canes, crutches, or walkers to visit museums or historic sites; they may use wheelchairs, or they may be subject to easy exhaustion. Some have birth defects; others, illnesses such as arthritis, polio, muscular dystrophy, or multiple sclerosis; and still others may have injuries from accidents or military service. Some have had heart or lung conditions or strokes; some have recovered from surgery for cancer or diabetes. Some, especially older people, may have uncertain balance, be unable to walk long distances, or be aware that they could easily break bones should they fall. All of them have difficulty with indoor and outdoor distances, uneven walk surfaces, and curbs, steps, and stairs.

There are 1.3 million blind persons in the United States, and 8.2 million more with limited vision. Although some of them fit the stereotype of the blind man finding his way with a cane or a guide dog and experiencing the world entirely by touch or hearing, 90 percent of those who are legally blind have some residual sight. Blindness may be caused by birth defects, by illnesses like glaucoma or diabetes, by injury or aging. Visual impairments may include extreme near- or far-sightedness, color-blindness, blurring vision, or inability to read small print. Although most blind persons do not also have limitations of mobility, they are likely to be concerned about falling or tripping over objects they cannot see, while some have a fear of heights. Such visitors appreciate exhibits simply designed, adequately lighted, and boldly labeled, with directions to objects they wish to look at and opportunities to touch them.

Deafness has been called the severest of all disabilities because it cuts a person off from language and ideas, as well as from sound. Such isolation is of course much more true of those who were born deaf than of those who have become so later in life through illness, accident, or aging. In the United States, there are 2.4 million deaf people and 11 million more with impaired hearing. Many of them use hearing aids, some communicate by lip reading or manual sign language, and all rely much upon the written word. They use their eyes to help or to substitute for their ears, and when they cannot see, communication is lost. They will gain much from persons trained to speak clearly and distinctly, as well as from sign language interpretation and appropriate printed materials.

Many people with mental limitations live in a world of direct sense impressions and close familiar associations, with little awareness of abstract ideas or remote times and places. They include 6.5 million mentally retarded, persons with mental illnesses or emotional disturbances, and children with such learning disabilities as dyslexia. Many of these conditions produce a short attention span, a tendency to become easily distracted, or inappropriate behavior. The more severely disabled museum visitors will probably come in groups supervised by personnel familiar with and to them, who can give museum staff members a good idea what to expect. But others, especially children "mainstreamed" into regular public school classes, may appear as members of ordinary groups. They need brief, concrete, and simple presentations, opportunities to use all their senses, and immediate approval of any expressions of interest.

Although many of America's 20 million elderly people are not disabled, the majority of handicapped persons are over sixty-five. They have all the preceding types of disabilities, some of which are caused and many of which are intensified by the processes of aging. Groups of elderly people may include some who are not disabled and others with varying degrees of disability, so that activities intended for them need to be fully accessible to avoid inadvertently excluding some members. Many of the nation's 1.7 million homebound and 2.1 million institutionalized citizens are also elderly. For them, visits to a museum or historical society's facilities may be impracticable, even if the premises are fully accessible, although some residential institutions have volunteers and transportation for occasional participation in community activities. Older people in general benefit from ample opportunities to sit down, from removal of such obstacles as uneven walk surfaces and steep and slippery stairs, and from outreach programs to take the society's resources to them.

It needs to be emphasized at this point that, though many elderly people are handicapped, age itself is in no way a disability. A number of historical societies answering survey questions on that subject stressed that they considered their older members and volunteers among their greatest assets. That is as it should be, for the long-time residents of any community are a part of its living history. Their interest in the historical society will help immeasurably with that organization's fundamental task of preserving traditions from the past as a firm foundation for building for future generations. Those who are disabled in some ways may yet have much to contribute in others and may be eager to do so if they are given the opportunity. Museums and historical organizations may therefore reap rich rewards by making sure that all older members of the community can participate in any available programs that interest them.

Although few disabled people have participated in historical society activities in the past, there is no reason to suppose them less interested in their local heritage than are people in general. They may have been prevented from coming forward by inaccessible facilities and programs, or they may be unaware of those that are accessible because the society has not mentioned such programs or facilities in its publicity. Or they may be kept away by other factors, such as inadequate transportation. Disabled persons who live independently may have to expend so much time and effort on the necessities of everyday living that they have little energy or resources to spare for leisure activities. Those who are cared for by others may have little opportunity to choose the activities of most interest to themselves.

These difficulties suggest some of the reasons why, so far, most disabled visitors come to historic sites or museums in groups and why nearly all of these groups come from special schools. Many of these special schools are private schools. Most of these groups come from schools for handicapped children and are thus provided with appropriate transportation and are accompanied by persons familiar with their needs and able to provide such special services as signed interpretation for the deaf. Organizations with accessible facilities have also discovered that it is necessary to publicize that fact and not merely to assume that disabled visitors will come if they wish. Handicapped people have learned by long experience to take for granted that public places are inaccessible to them unless the contrary is explicitly stated. Many historical organization staff members overestimate the difficulty of serving these people because they envision all disabilities in their severest form. But there is no sharp line between handicapped people on the one side and normal people on the other: rather, there is a wide range of varying degrees of impairment. What disabled persons need is not so much programs designed especially for the handicapped as adjustments that will in many cases substantially improve the service of a museum or historic organization for its general audience.

"I Don't Know What Section 504 Is"

A number of survey respondents were unfamiliar with the sequence of events that made "Section 504" a household word to handicapped persons and a source of concern to organizations serving the public of which they are a part. A vigorous protest movement by disabled people convinced that they were being denied the equal protection of the laws prompted Congress to pass the Rehabilitation Act of 1973 (P.L. 93–112). Section 504 of this law is a basic civil rights statement prohibiting discrimination against any person by reason of his handicap by any organization receiving federal financial support. The first set of guidelines for compliance with Section 504 was issued by the Department of Health, Education, and Welfare in May 1977. These HEW guidelines have served as a model for directives of many other federal agencies including the National Endowment for the Arts.

All these guidelines prohibit discrimination against handicapped persons in employment and insist that facilities and programs be made accessible to them within a stated period, warning that neither trouble nor expense will be accepted as excuses for noncompliance. Their express purpose is to integrate disabled people into existing programs; the establishment of separate programs that would tend to perpetuate their segregation is not acceptable. Section 504 is of particular concern to museums and historical organizations that have already received or intend to apply for grants from NEA or the new HEW Office of Museum Services. Smaller organizations often believe they are not covered because they receive no federal funds; but the regulations also apply to federal money distributed through state and local governments. This includes both revenue-sharing and the wages of the CETA employees who make many of their programs possible.

There is much misunderstanding of the Section 504 guidelines. They do not require affirmative-action employment, major reconstruction of existing buildings, or immediate compliance. Instead, they require that an organization appoint a responsible staff member to ascertain whether handicapped persons can participate in the organization's program when viewed in its entirety. The organization must also review employment practices for discrimination, prepare a "transition plan" if structural modifications are necessary, and include disabled individuals and groups in the planning of alterations intended for their benefit. The central requirement of all these regulations is *program* accessibility. The NEA guidelines state explicitly that structural alteration is to be undertaken only as a last resort if significant parts of the organization's program cannot be made available to disabled persons in any other way.

Curators of historic buildings quickly recognized a conflict between the requirement that they accommodate the handicapped under Section 504 and their obligation to preserve the historical and architectural integrity of these structures under the Historic Preservation Act of 1966. The Department of the Interior, which administers many historic sites through the National Park Service, issued guidelines to resolve this contradiction in April 1979. These guidelines state that accessibility at historic properties shall be achieved in a manner consistent with their historical and architectural integrity. Architectural modifications shall be undertaken only when all other possible means have been exhausted. Suggested alternatives include building new facilities, such as visitor centers, or conducting part of the program in other, more accessible locations, assigning personnel to assist disabled individuals, or devising other methods. The National Advisory Council on Historic Preservation, established in 1966 to protect the interests of properties listed on the National Register of Historic Places, has recently issued recommended language on accessibility at historic sites, which includes the possibility of case-by-case waivers as a last resort in the rare instances where no alternative can be devised without damage to their historical integrity. This language, however, has not yet been adopted by any federal funding agency, and the principle of waivers is challenged by some disabled civil rights groups, so all museums, historical societies, state-based historical agencies, and other historically oriented organizations will need to keep abreast of further developments in this controversy.

Many historical museums, art museums, and historically related organizations find the Section 504 guidelines confusing because their language was intended to cover a wide range of circumstances, many of which may never arise in small institutions. But when the simple thrust of these regulations is restated in terms appropriate to the actual activities of such organizations, it may be seen that they are really very practical. For example, it is common sense that one person be designated co-ordinator of activities for disabled persons, with responsibility for securing information, completing the necessary forms, and seeing that other staff members and volunteers work together to carry out proposed changes. Consultation with disabled persons can also save a great deal of time and trouble and may prevent costly mistakes. The required "self-evaluation" and "transition plan" are intended to be written statements of the institution's present accessibility and of an orderly set of steps for implementing any structural alterations that prove to be unavoidable. The co-ordinator and advisory committee of disabled persons will then need to review these plans at intervals to be sure that the steps are being accomplished on schedule to meet the 1982 deadline.

Many historical organizations fear that compliance with Section 504 will require a disproportionate diversion of their limited resources. That is not the intention of the guidelines, which require the integration of handicapped persons into *existing* programs. Many procedures mandated by the guidelines may actually increase the effectiveness of museums' and historical organizations' general operations. To determine how a program in its entirety can be made available to disabled persons, it may be necessary to define that program and its purpose. Consulting with handicapped persons may bring an organization into contact with important members of its community who have not previously been interested in that institution's activities. Achievement of program accessibility and efforts to raise funds for structural modifications may give the organization a golden opportunity to enhance its public image as an institution concerned about the community as a whole.

Museums and historical organizations can begin assessing program accessibility by asking whether persons with limited mobility can enter the facility, what parts of it they can reach, and which program activities conducted in inaccessible areas could be rescheduled elsewhere. Audiovisual interpretation may be an appropriate alternative for the upper stories of historic buildings. When program adjustments are completed, the unavoidable structural modifications may prove to be much less formidable than was at first supposed. It is also important to consider how exhibits, publication, and research facilities can be made available to persons with limited vision. Those with limited hearing may wish to attend lectures and films as well as orientation presentations and guided tours. Visitors with mental limitations may gain a great deal from museum experiences adapted to their level of comprehension.

The needs of the disabled may also suggest worthwhile new directions for the historical institution's activities. Outreach programs to take audiovisual presentations and sample artifacts to schools are equally appropriate for senior citizens' centers, nursing homes, and residential facilities for the severely disabled. Service organizations may arrange tours for groups of people who have never had an opportunity to visit a museum. Some radio reading services for the blind already use local history materials and would welcome the assistance of the historical society in selecting more of them. Some older citizens, including residents of nursing homes, can make valuable contributions to oral history projects. And handicapped individuals will find ways to use the society's resources that neither they nor anyone else had dreamed of.

"We Hadn't Really Thought Much about It"

Although a growing body of literature presents ways in which museums could meet the needs of disabled visitors, very little is known about what small organizations are actually doing or about the obstacles they find in their way. To provide some definite information on this subject, a survey questionnaire was sent to 750 organizational members of the American Association for State and Local History, 733 of them in the United States and 17 in Canada. Of these questionnaires, 286, nearly 40 percent, were returned from forty-five states and two Canadian provinces, an unusually high response to a mail survey. They revealed a number of historical societies with well-developed programming for handicapped persons, a few who were emphatically not interested, and many who had been putting off the whole issue for fear of what it might involve.

Follow-up letters to 160 of them requesting further information elicited 61 replies. Although a few of them admitted that they had been confused and did not in fact provide the services indicated, most described activities showing a high degree of imagination and ingenuity in meeting the needs of at least some of their local handicapped audience. The complete tabulation of the survey and examples of these programs, illustrating their great variety, will be found in Appendixes B and C of this book.

Several questions concerned the general characteristics of these societies, such as their size, with reference to which the results were tabulated. There were 51 (17 percent) with less than 200 members; 104 (35 percent) with 200 to 500 members; 68 (23 percent) with 500 to 1,000 members; 47 (16 percent) with more than 1,000 members; and 16 (5 percent) who did not respond to this query. Nearly half of them, including most of the smallest, have been founded since 1950; nearly one third, earlier in the twentieth century; and the remainder, in the nineteenth, mostly in the years surrounding the national centennial of 1876, though a few, including some of the largest, date from before the Civil War. Nearly one-third, including more than half of those with less than 500 members, focus upon the history of a town or city. Nearly half, including two-thirds of those with 500 to 1,000 members, cover a county. About one-tenth include several counties, while about one-sixth, of whom some are among the largest societies responding, cover their entire states.

The most widespread program activities of these societies are museums and guided tours. The three-quarters of them that operate museums include nine-tenths of those with 200 to 1,000 members. These range from one or two rooms in the society's headquarters or a historic house open a few days a year to large, open-gallery museums and outdoor complexes of historic structures. Guided tours are sponsored by two-thirds, including four-fifths of those with 200 to 1,000 members. Many of these are showings of historic houses that no visitors are permitted to enter without a guide. A few are walking tours or bus tours of historic districts, some of which have been very ingeniously adapted to the needs of special groups.

Also numerous are societies maintaining research libraries and publication programs. The two-thirds that have such libraries include three-quarters of those with more than 500 members. Holdings of the libraries themselves range from a few hundred books and cartons of uncatalogued documents—stored in the headquarters attic and almost inaccessible to anyone—to major research collections staffed by professional librarians and frequently used by scholars as well as society members. The two-thirds that produce some sort of publications include four-fifths of those with more than 500 members. They bring out books and pamphlets commemorating community anniversaries—particularly the bicentennial—continuing series of volumes collecting local lore, and a number of scholarly journals. Some smaller societies, however, made a point of the fact that their publications are limited to brochures and newsletters.

Two-thirds of these organizations, including four-fifths of those with 200 to 1,000 members, extend their activities into the community by means of organized educational programs. Most of these consist of tours of the museum by public school field trips, but some are also designed for adults, particularly members of special populations. One-third, including most of those with more than 1,000 members, also sponsor outreach programs to take historical society resources to such groups in their own locations. Starting with school classes, they have often been extended to senior citizens' centers, nursing homes, and residential facilities for the severely disabled. Special events such as lectures, films, and concerts take place at two-thirds, particularly three-quarters of those with more than 500 members. Some occur in regular series, while others mark annual anniversaries of local events or occasions of general celebration, such as Christmas or the Fourth of July.

A more recently developed area of interest is historic preservation, important to two-thirds of these societies, notably three-quarters of those with less than 1,000 members. These range from groups founded to purchase and restore a local landmark to an organization of residents of an urban historic district covering a considerable area. In some instances, the emphasis on preservation may have developed from an older concern with marking historic sites, which is still practiced by one-third of these societies. A few indicated that their members have a special interest in genealogy. Others are beginning to collect tape recordings for the preservation of oral history. One or two in areas with strong traditions of local crafts are documenting crafts on slides, videotape, and film, as well as collecting the articles the craftsmen produce.

Some organizations occupy a single building, but many have more than one, and a number own substantial amounts of real estate. About one quarter, including half of those with more than 500 members, have a headquarters building; and about one quarter have a separate museum, but only a few have a separate library. Some of the smaller institutions rent rooms in public buildings that also house other organizations required to provide access for disabled persons. Others lease facilities where alterations are the responsibility of the owner. The largest societies also maintain a variety of miscellaneous structures, such as art galleries, crafts workshops, and summer theaters. The different types of problems they present for disabled people include occasional access for individual and group visits, regular accommodations for disabled employees, and arrangements for safe participation by handicapped persons in public assemblies.

Two-thirds of these societies must face the peculiar access problems presented by historic structures. Of the two-fifths that own historic houses, most have only one, but a number own more than one. The one-fifth that have other types of buildings are divided about evenly between those with one and those with more than one. There are also 15 (5 percent) with museum villages. They represent a very wide variety of structures, such as churches, schools, Indian missions, jails, forts, mills, mines, factories, and warehouses. Some unusual items associated with transportation are railroad stations and rolling stock, steamboats, sailing vessels, a dredge, and a lighthouse. About one quarter are in officially designated historic districts, while 5 percent specify that they are on the National Register of Historic Places.

More than half of these societies employ full-time and one-third employ part-time professional staff. Most have only

The Nebraska State Historical Society's dredge *Captain Meriwether Lewis,* at Brownville, Nebraska, is being made accessible to disabled visitors.— *Courtesy Nebraska State Historical Society*

one or two—a director who must be all things to all people, with the help of a librarian, curatorial, educational, or general assistant. Only the larger societies have more numerous staff, which permits specialization. Two-fifths use full-time and one-third use part-time nonprofessional employees; most of them use only one or two, but a few have as many as twenty-five. These include directors and librarians without special training, in the smaller societies, as well as secretarial and maintenance personnel in the larger ones. The very few employees who are handicapped have a wide range of disabilities: there are amputees, arthritics, people with multiple sclerosis, polio, visual impairment, and a few who use wheelchairs.

Most of these societies rely heavily—and some rely entirely—on volunteers. About half use volunteers as guides, and about one-third use them in other capacities, in numbers ranging from a few to more than a hundred. Especially in smaller societies, volunteer directors, librarians, editors of newsletters, and chairmen of fund-raising or guides committees may differ from semiprofessionals only in that they donate their services. A number have a few handicapped volunteers, again with the full range of disabilities, including some instances of mental limitation. There was some confusion about whether older people in general should be included in the "disabled" group, and several emphasized that they relied heavily on older volunteers and did not consider them disabled. Indeed, they could hardly exist without them, particularly for tasks requiring more time and continuity than younger members could spare from their jobs and family responsibilities.

The most substantial form of federal assistance received by these organizations is the wages of CETA employees, reported by two-fifths, in amounts commonly ranging between $10,000 and $50,000. One-quarter have received federal revenue-sharing monies distributed through their state and local governments, and about one-tenth have obtained federal funds for architectural restoration. One-tenth have received grants from the National Endowment for the Humanities, 6 percent from the National Endowment for the Arts, and 3 percent from the new HEW Office of Museum Services, but none from the National Science Foundation. Although many societies did not choose to tell how much they received from these sources, the amounts reported ranged from less than $2,500 to $1,250,000. Recipients of the larger direct grants were most aware of their responsibilities under Section 504, and most of them are actively developing projects to fulfill them. Small organizations, especially those that benefit indirectly through CETA or revenue-sharing programs, are much more likely to be confused and concerned about what is expected of them.

Most of these organizations think of accommodation for handicapped individuals primarily in terms of access to their facilities. Two-thirds have at least one building that persons with limited mobility can approach and enter without impediment; one-fifth have more than one. One-fourth reported that such visitors could reach all floors of at least one building. Most of these buildings are modern headquarters, libraries, or museums, but some historic facilities are all on one floor, and a very few contain elevators. One-sixth claim to have alternative interpretation of inaccessible areas, but follow-up inquiries revealed that many of them had been confused by the term. Some instruct guides to describe rooms to those who cannot reach them, a few have slides or pictures, and one has prepared a videotape for this purpose.

Adjustments needed by persons with limited vision have been much less widely adopted. Large-type labels are used in one-eighth, but only a few have printed their brochures in that form, and almost none have either labels or brochures available in Braille or recorded cassettes. Many, however, permit blind persons to touch objects, and some have special tours for the blind, sponsored by organizations such as the Lions Club. One-tenth are willing to provide assistance to visually limited persons in using catalogues and other library materials, but nearly all of them report that there has been no demand for this service, perhaps because users do not know it is available. A few have arrangements to record local history materials, usually through a state or regional library for the blind. One that has worked with the local radio station for the blind reports that historical programs have been very well received.

Likewise, only scattered historical organizations have installed electronic amplification for persons with impaired hearing or instructed their guides how to speak to those who lip-read. Most of the one-sixth who have printed materials available for the deaf use their regular publications for that purpose. A few have experimented with sign-language interpretation or, more commonly, worked with interpreters accompanying deaf groups. One-eighth serve mentally retarded groups, usually from schools, sheltered workshops, or local centers. They usually adapt their regular tours for that purpose by simplifying and shortening them. The same approach is commonly used with groups of mental patients, children with learning disabilities, or people with other mental limitations.

Most of the organizations that have taken formal steps to comply with Section 504 guidelines have already received considerable amounts of federal funds. One-eighth of those responding to the survey have appointed a staff member to serve as compliance officer; in most instances, the compliance officer responded to the questionnaire. Only 6 percent have invited handicapped individuals and the agencies that serve them to act as an advisory committee. One-quarter, however, have completed the process of needs assessment and self-evaluation. About one-tenth have implemented program adaptations, prepared a "transition plan" for structural modifications, and reviewed employment procedures for discrimination. A question about the role of the board of directors in these activities was much misunderstood, but follow-up replies indicated that most changes have been initiated by the organization's staff.

Even though most museums and historical organizations have not yet appointed advisory committees, many are in fact already working with handicapped groups in their communities. Senior citizens' centers were the most widely reported, having developed programs with about one-third of the societies. These include councils for the aging and R.S.V.P. chapters, one of which is conducting an accessibility survey of local buildings, some of which are of historic importance. About one-tenth have co-operated with social service agencies and organizations of handicapped persons, and fewer with rehabilitation centers and residential facilities. These organizations cover a full range of disabilities, and include schools for the blind and the deaf, sheltered workshops, and centers for the mentally ill and the mentally retarded. Such activities are by no means entirely in response to present-day concerns, for some of them have been going on for a long time—one for forty years and another for sixty years.

Very few of these organizations have made any effort to publicize their accessible features. Less than one-tenth mention them in their brochures or through local media coverage of special events involving handicapped groups. Almost none feature them in advertising, partly because, as many pointed out, they do not advertise at all. About two-fifths are affiliated with state historical associations, and about one-third with regional consortia, but only 7 percent reported that these bodies provided any advice or assistance in meeting the needs of disabled persons. A few had learned much at workshops sponsored by such organizations, but the very large number of responses saying "Don't know of any" to that question might suggest to such groups that more publicity for *their* efforts is needed.

The most widely cited obstacle in the way of improving accessibility is lack of funds, reported by half the groups surveyed, who went on to tell of the tightness of their budgets and the other economies being forced upon them. Nearly half pointed to insufficient staff, particularly when financial stringency is dictating reductions in personnel. One-quarter indicate inaccessible facilities, and one-sixth mention inadequate information. Some of the one-third who think there is little interest among the handicapped have tried to consult or invite local agencies without response. Of the one-seventh who find no interest among the nonhandicapped, some give the impression it is within their own organization, especially if it is small, recently established, or preoccupied with an expensive and time-consuming project such as saving and restoring a historic landmark. Others, however, make clear that this insensitivity is in the community at large, giving examples of indifferent local governments and disinterested state agencies whose support—not necessarily financial—is needed.

Only a scattering of historically related organizations report programs specifically for persons with various disabilities, but many more indicate that they do their best to accommodate such visitors within the framework of their existing activities—which is far closer to what the Section 504 guidelines actually require. One society in the midwest invited a group of nursing-home patients in wheelchairs to tour its museum after their Christmas dinner at a senior citizens' center in the same building and entertained them at its holiday exhibit of old-time decorations featuring carols played on a historic church organ by costumed volunteers. Another, in an eastern state, sponsors an annual evening when members of the local Lions Club bring blind persons and their relatives to tour the museum, where display cases are opened so that the visitors may touch anything. In conjunction with the bicentennial, still another eastern society prepared a sign-language tour that was eventually enjoyed by a large proportion of the deaf people in its area. Retarded children, along with other school groups, learn to participate in traditional Appalachian crafts at a historical society museum in the South. Older residents of a northern New England town have turned their old schoolhouse, now owned by the historical society, into a thriving senior citizens' center that has attracted considerable attention and financial support by its efficient assistance with the needs of the elderly, thus perpetuating the tradition of self-reliance and mutual help characteristic of New England.

This survey therefore suggests that most museums and historical organizations have far less to worry about than many of them fear in meeting their legal and moral obligation to include handicapped persons in their general audience. Most are aware of the necessity for improving access to persons with limited mobility, and some have done so already. Although many believe that adjustments for persons with visual handicaps and hearing and mental limitations are beyond their reach, a number have demonstrated that that is not necessarily so difficult. The contributions of older people can, with some thought, be extended to include those who are disabled. Some organizations found that the questionnaire itself gave them ideas and relieved their anxieties about what the law required of them. It is hoped that the chapters that follow will be of further help.

2

"Things We Can Do Right Now"

MANY community organizations are concerned about the impact of Section 504 because they have heard of it primarily through media coverage of protest demonstrations by handicapped militants. Like members of other minorities, disabled Americans have called attention to their demands for changes in the conditions of their lives by organizing a vigorous civil rights movement. The passage of the Rehabilitation Act of 1973 and the issuance of the first guidelines for compliance with Section 504 were at least partly prompted by wheelchair marches in Washington and sit-ins at HEW offices all over the country. Disabled individuals and groups have brought a number of suits under the Architectural Barriers Act of 1968 against inaccessible public facilities, including various types of cultural organizations. Some theaters and museums, fearing adverse publicity, have settled such suits out of court by undertaking hastily designed structural modifications, such as elevators, which have sometimes been more costly than was really necessary. Others fear that should such an issue be raised, the cost might be so great as to force them to cease operation, thus depriving everyone of pleasures all would like to enjoy.

Museums and historically related organizations are particularly vulnerable to that type of threat. Most are small, locally based organizations working on tight budgets with slender resources, little outside support, and few reserves. Many of them think that accommodations for the handicapped mean the installation of a ramp or an elevator that would cost more than their entire annual expenditure. Or perhaps they have been organized to preserve historic structures where such alterations could not be made without damaging the building's historical and architectural integrity. One such director responded to the survey, with astonished gratitude, "Your questionnaire suggested a lot of simple things we can do right now." That organization has already started to do some of those things; this chapter may suggest ways in which others can do likewise.

"A Board of Directors Who Support Such Efforts"

The first essential element in any program planned for disabled persons by any museum or historical organization is the backing of its board of directors. Sometimes the initiative may come from staff members made aware of Section 504 regulations through their efforts to secure federal funds; but in smaller societies the impetus in this, as in other matters, may come from the president, members of the board, or chairmen of volunteer committees. However the organization functions, action of the board will be necessary to raise and expend funds and to mobilize human resources. A clear and cogent statement of policy and of the reasons for it is therefore necessary. Such a statement may be drafted by the staff, debated and passed by the board, and disseminated to the entire membership.

It is important for anyone preparing such statements to remember how many other matters the board of directors have to concern them. The agenda of a typical meeting may include the problem of urgent repairs needed by a historic house, negotiations with the local government for continued support, reappraisal of the collection for insurance purposes, and recruiting of volunteer guides to conduct a new program of tours for school children. The members of the board, furthermore, are busy people from a wide variety of backgrounds who participate in historically related activities as only one of many community responsibilities. In the course of these other activities, they may have become aware of the necessity of complying with Section 504, and they may be genuinely eager to welcome their disabled fellow-citizens to the society. But they are not concerned about the details of how that is to be done, nor is a regular, monthly general meeting an efficient place to arrange specific courses of action. The statement they are asked to debate, amend, and approve should therefore be clear and brief and should be presented without lengthy explanation.

If the organization is small, the board may wish to appoint an ad hoc committee of its own members, and perhaps interested volunteers, to draw up its statement of policy. The first thing such a committee will need to determine is whether the organization is obligated to comply with Section 504. It is so obligated if it receives funds from any federal agency or from state arts or humanities councils supported by federal funds. If the organization receives federal money through a state or local government, such as revenue-sharing grants or funds for CETA employees, it should check with officials of that government to see whether it is required to comply. If funds from federal projects contribute to overhead, general operating expense, or administrative salaries, then the entire program must comply with Section 504; if not, then only those projects need comply. Some states now also require compliance with Section 504 for recipients of state funds.

If the organization falls into any of those groups, then its *ad hoc* committee will need to draft a resolution embodying the organization's intention to provide equal treatment for handicapped persons. This means that disabled persons must have the same opportunities as anyone else to enter the organization's facilities, participate in its program, and secure employment. Insofar as possible, disabled people are to be integrated into existing activities, rather than segregated in special ones. It is not necessary, however, to provide access to every square foot of the organization's facilities or to every event, if representative parts of the program, viewed in its entirety, are available to disabled individuals. The resolution should also indicate the institution's intention to call that fact to the attention of disabled persons in its publicity. The resolution should be brief—a paragraph supported by not more than a page of explanation—and after approval by the board, it should be communicated to all members and their participation in carrying it out invited.

The same committee may then proceed to review the organization's employment practices for evidence of discrimination. It should be emphasized that Section 504, while forbidding discrimination, does not require affirmative action in employment. Therefore the society is not expected to go out of its way to recruit disabled employees, to alter basic job descriptions, or to create positions that do not exist. What it does mean is that an organization cannot discriminate against a handicapped person if he or she is the best-qualified applicant for a position that must be filled. Positions and job descriptions must be fully advertised in a variety of media, including those available to persons with limited vision or hearing. Interviewing and pre-employment examinations must also be free of discrimination.

The committee must realize, however, that they may be required to make certain adjustments necessary for disabled employees to do their jobs. That could involve reassigning office space, redefining responsibilities or work schedules, or providing suitable equipment or assistance, such as readers or interpreters. It will clearly be easier to make such accommodations in large institutions than in small ones, which may find that they create undue hardship. If that should indeed be true, the failure to hire or promote a handicapped person will not be regarded as discriminatory. Nevertheless, many such accommodations are in fact far less trouble and expense than might be anticipated, so they should be very carefully considered before dismissing the possibility. It is also important to note that equal opportunity does not require special treatment, such as exceptions to rules applied to all employees forbidding the use of alcohol or drugs on the job.

Survey respondents—some of them quite small—with disabled employees made it quite clear that the contributions of these employees far outweighed any inconveniences caused by their disabilities. A disabled director at one organization is responsible for an outstanding program of accommodation for handicapped visitors, based on unusual insight into their real needs. An exhibit preparator in a state museum finds his wheelchair no impediment to working in any part of the building. Some valuable suggestions on designing exhibits that can be enjoyed by persons with limited vision came from a curator with that impairment. Two historical societies had volunteers with cerebral palsy who have since become employees; one is now working in a clerical capacity and the other plans to make a career of museum work. Another society found that a retarded clerical worker required more supervision than its staff could provide and wished for greater liaison with the agency that had prepared that individual for work in an unsheltered setting.

"Many Things We Do Are Just Common Sense"

Many museums and historically related organizations have discovered that examining their programs with reference to accessibility will in itself suggest a number of simple but effective adjustments. First, the co-ordinator needs to become better informed by securing copies of Section 504 guidelines and supporting literature from appropriate federal agencies—NEA, NEH, the HEW Office of Museum Services, and the National Science Foundation, as well as state and local building codes and copies of laws and ordinances prohibiting discrimination against disabled individuals. Some of the growing body of literature concerning compliance with these regulations is discussed in the bibliographic essay of this book. Of particular importance are the publications of the National Information Service for Arts and the Handicapped (ARTS). Every museum and historically related organization should subscribe to this series of technical pamphlets on all aspects of the subject. They may be secured free of charge from ARTS, Arts and Special Constituencies Program, National Endowment for the Arts, 2401 E Street N.W., Washington, D.C. 20506.

The co-ordinator will also want to make a preliminary assessment of the accessibility of the institution's program and facilities. A "Needs Assessment Survey Instrument" for that purpose is available from ARTS. This detailed questionnaire includes sections on eligibility, organizational aspects, employment practices, program activities, and architectural barriers. It was designed for a wide range of organizations of all sizes in the performing as well as the visual arts. The small museum or historical society may find it somewhat overwhelming at first sight, and some of its questions may seem inapplicable. But it is a good place to start, because it gives an excellent idea of what the regulations do and do not expect.

The first point emphasized by this document and by all the literature on the subject is that the guidelines require accessibility of *programs,* rather than facilities. This means that if the organization's program, when viewed in its entirety, can be made available to handicapped persons without structural

Both ground-level and first-floor entrances are accessible to wheelchair visitors at this Eaton, Ohio, museum housed in a former "bank barn," built originally with a "banked" ramp at first-floor level so that wagons could enter.—*Courtesy Preble County (O.) Historical Society*

modifications, no such modifications are necessary. That situation can sometimes be brought about by rescheduling activities in parts of the building where disabled individuals can attend them. The requirement is, further, that facilities be "accessible," rather than "barrier-free." "Barrier-free" means that a handicapped person can enter by any doorway, reach all floors, and use all public amenities such as rest rooms, telephones, and water fountains. "Accessible" means that a disabled person can enter by at least one doorway, reach important areas, and use some public amenities.

It should also be emphasized that the intent of the regulations is to integrate disabled persons, insofar as possible, into the historical organization's existing program. Separate activities for particular groups are not prohibited, but they are not in themselves sufficient to comply with the law. This means that a full range of activities must be conducted in locations that persons with limited mobility can reach. Equipment or interpretation needs to be provided so that those with limited vision or hearing can enjoy exhibits and special events alongside others. Staff members and volunteers need to be trained in techniques for assisting disabled individuals as well as dealing with special groups. And the organization's publicity should call attention to the accessibility of its programs through a variety of media, including special networks such as newsletters for the deaf and radio stations for the blind.

Visits to museums and guided tours of historic sites are the program activities most frequently reported by the historical societies surveyed. The first question to be asked about these places is whether persons with limited mobility can approach and enter them. Where can they park, and what is the shortest route to the entrance with the fewest steps? Inside the building, are doorways and halls wide enough to accommodate a wheelchair and is furniture arranged to provide unobstructed passage? Are exhibits and displays visible from a seated as well as from a standing position, and are there opportunities for persons with limited strength to sit down? Can one reach all floors of the building, or will that require structural modifications or alternative interpretation?

Parking spaces for handicapped drivers should be as close as possible to the building and should be designated by the international accessibility symbol. Signs for that purpose are often available without charge from the state department of transportation. If parking is on the street and the institution is open only at certain times, portable signs may be used so that the reserved space will be available for others when the building is closed. In parking lots, one out of fifty spaces should be so designated. They need to be twelve feet wide, so that the car door can be fully opened to enable a person to transfer to a wheelchair positioned beside the car. It may therefore be convenient to arrange these spaces at the end of a row, but persons who move slowly should not be expected to get out of a car into a stream of passing traffic.

Curb cuts are also needed at all curbs between the parking area and the historical institution's entrance. On public streets, the municipality will often install them free of charge; one is needed at each end of the block, as well as near a reserved parking space. If the organization wishes to install curb cuts on its own property, the most effective kind cuts away the curb and slopes the sidewalk gently to street level. Filling in the space between sidewalk and street with asphalt may create a number of hazards and can interfere with drainage. A slightly roughened surface, such as two rows of bricks laid end to end, will warn blind persons using canes of an approaching intersection. Suggested designs may be found in "Curb Cuts for the Handicapped: Draft Blueprints" (available from the Architectural and Transportation Barriers Compliance Commission, Washington, D.C. 20201).

The most accessible entrance to the building is almost always that with the fewest steps. (Overcoming these steps by means of a ramp or lift is a structural modification to be discussed in the next chapter.) In new buildings, disabled persons understandably expect that the main entrance will accommodate them with the rest of the general public; but in historic structures, that is not always possible, especially when the building's front portico is of historic or architectural significance. The route to that entrance from the parking lot and the nearest bus stop should be clearly marked with the international symbol. Walk surfaces need to be smooth, firm, and in good repair. If sections of a public sidewalk are broken or frost-heaved, the municipality can be asked to replace them as a matter of safety for everyone.

Most historical society buildings have doors wide enough (thirty-six inches) to accommodate standard wheelchairs. It may be possible for a wheelchair pushed by someone to pass through a narrower historic door; but if that is not possible, the society may wish to consider purchasing a narrower wheelchair for the use of visitors, or it may have to devise alternative interpretation. It is well to make sure that hallways are unobstructed and that rooms are uncluttered by furniture. If the arrangement of pieces is historic, much can often be accomplished by shifting some of them by just a few inches. Floors need to be smooth, and small rugs are dangerous to persons on crutches, as well as impediments to those in wheelchairs. The rubber or plastic runners sometimes used to protect floors or historic carpets should have non-skid surfaces and should be taped down securely at the sides as well as the ends.

Persons with difficulty in walking also appreciate ample opportunities to sit down and continue to appreciate the collection while they rest. Museums with galleries need in each room at least one substantial chair with arms. The chair should, preferably, be placed against a wall so that it cannot skid backward when someone leans on it in sitting or rising. The seat should not be too low, or it may be difficult for those who need it most to use it. Backless benches and the folding canvas stools available in some major museums may be dangerous, because they do not provide adequate support. In some historic rooms, there may be chairs suitable for this purpose—it has been suggested that occasional use might even be good for them, as well as making the rooms seem more homelike. If the chair's upholstery or construction make it too delicate for use, appropriate reproductions might be provided.

Organizations that arrange exhibits behind glass will find that vertical rather than horizontal cases are much more convenient for children, as well as for persons who use wheelchairs; the line of sight of a person seated in a wheelchair is about eighteen inches below that of a standing adult. Small or particularly significant artifacts should be placed at or near a viewer's-eye level and the space above used for objects that may be appreciated from a distance. Since it is awkward and tiring to look continuously sideways over one's shoulder, sufficient space between cases needs to be provided for a person in a wheelchair to turn and face any objects he particularly wishes to study. One or two clamp-on mirrors for wheelchairs, available for persons who have difficulty in lifting or turning their heads, might also be a worthwhile investment. Accessible arrangement of showcases and literature racks is further important in the gift shop. The illuminated tray of slides will be low enough for a person in a wheelchair to make selections if it is on a counter over which he or she can see the salesperson.

If it is difficult to lower the water fountain to a height comfortable for wheelchair users, a dispenser of paper cups and a wastebasket can be placed beside the fountain. A long stick can be attached to the fountain's framework, to permit the foot pedal to be depressed by hand. Many people are not aware that the telephone company will lower public telephones at no cost. Electronic amplification equipment for persons with impaired hearing is also available without charge. It is further important to be sure that telephone booths are wide enough for a person in a wheelchair to enter and that there is, inside the booth, a shelf to support heavy directories when in use. Small historic houses that permit visitors to use the phone at the information desk can make it accessible to disabled persons by attaching a long cord.

Many accommodations important to persons with limited vision and hearing are equally simple and inexpensive. Some museums type labels for individual objects on a large-type typewriter, which a historical society can borrow from a local school or library for occasional use. The text of brochures can also be typed on such a machine and reproduced by offset printing. Labels for works of art can be more easily seen from a distance by everyone if the letters are five-eighths of an inch high, black on white or white on black. All exhibits need to be well lighted and designed with bold contrasts of color and shape, and the institution may wish to procure one or two large magnifying glasses for examining details.

Every museum and historical organization staff member and volunteer should have an opportunity to watch a blind person trained in the art of touching sweep his hands delicately over an object to perceive its contours and texture. Although some blind people insist that they do not wish to be singled out for special touching privileges, museums and historical societies have a good reason for making a distinction in policy between persons trained in this technique and the general public. Furthermore, a curator points out that museum staff members themselves never touch many rare objects without gloves, because even trace amounts of perspiration or body oils can set in motion destructive long-term chemical changes. Some museums therefore require blind visitors to wear gloves of rubber or thin fabric, but a worker with the blind points out that these gloves cause confusing distortions, and suggests instead that blind visitors be given an opportunity beforehand to wash and thoroughly dry their hands, perhaps in a warm-air blower. The curator insists that that is not sufficient and advises that advance arrangements be made, so that such objects can be touched only in the presence of a staff member prepared to clean them properly immediately afterward. Small museums may have some treasured pieces of silver, furniture, or paintings demanding that treatment, but many objects of daily use in olden times are not so delicate. But blind persons do not expect to touch everything, and there should be a definite policy concerning which objects may and may not be touched, under what circumstances.

Some art museums suggest that objects to be touched should be stably mounted and free from projecting points, but one history museum points out that visitors must still be led to them and it is better to select smaller artifacts that can be passed among the group. More time than usual must be allowed for this activity, so that each visitor will have ample opportunity to touch each artifact. Since some elderly people prefer to avoid standing for long periods, it may be wise to select several representative examples to be passed from hand to hand while the visitors are seated, before the tour. Some historic houses require all visitors to view historic rooms from behind a rope or gate at the door. A change in policy may be necessary to permit persons with limited vision to enter these rooms with a guide. It is reasonable to request advance notice for such visits so that they can be arranged for times when the house is not crowded, an arrangement that blind people themselves usually prefer.

Some simple adjustments may make the organization's research library much more available to disabled users. Besides needing access to the building, persons with limited mobility may need assistance in handling card catalog drawers and heavy books. If the library is on the second floor of a historic house, an index to the catalog and a desk might be provided on the first floor, to make it possible for readers who cannot climb the stairs to select and use catalog drawers and books that may be brought down to them. Those with limited vision may need help in skimming catalog cards and index entries for the items on which they wish to concentrate. Staff members may be able to spare a limited amount of time to get them started, and volunteer readers might be secured for those who give advance notice that they need more help. It would be well to post a conspicuous notice that such service is available; a number of historical societies surveyed noted that they would provide the service if asked, but indicated that, so far, there had been no requests.

Special events—lectures, films, concerts—are often held in an auditorium that should be accessible to persons with limited mobility. If such an auditorium is in the basement of a historic structure or is otherwise hopelessly inaccessible, it might be arranged for some scheduled events to take place elsewhere. If the auditorium is a multipurpose room where folding chairs are set up on such occasions, it is easy enough to leave wide aisles and move a few chairs to make room for wheelchairs. If the auditorium has fixed seats, it may be necessary to remove a few in convenient locations, keeping in mind that persons with limited mobility may also have limited vision or hearing and that they, like everyone else, wish to sit near the people with whom they attend the performance. It is not sufficient merely to make room for them in the back of the hall or to expect that they park in the aisles, where they would be a hazard to everyone in case of fire. The entire subject of including disabled patrons in general regulations for safety at places of public assembly requires further consideration, but it is clear that wheelchair locations need to be as close as possible to unimpeded exits from the auditorium and the building. Furthermore, staff fire drills should include practice in moving a wheelchair quickly and efficiently to the exit, and one staff person should be specifically assigned to that duty when handicapped persons are present in the audience.

Lectures and films may also need to be interpreted for deaf persons. It may be worthwhile to employ a professional sign-language interpreter for selected lectures. Deaf persons will particularly enjoy slide presentations if the interpreter is positioned at one side beneath a small light and the lecturer is warned not to change the slides too fast, so that observers have time to look from one to the other. Some feature films and some film presentations on historical subjects are available with captions, similar to the subtitles of those in foreign languages. One public library runs a regular series of such films, and historical organizations might wish to consider a similar program. Since deaf people have very few opportunities to participate in community entertainment, such a project would be most worthwhile, particularly if the films chosen appeal to a wide range of interests.

The historical society's education program is particularly likely to encounter handicapped children, because so many of them are now being "mainstreamed" in regular public school classes. Although some school officials believe it to be discriminating against such children to identify them, not doing so can make their visits difficult for museum guides who have to meet the special needs of variously handicapped young people without warning. The society can therefore include on its usual form for teachers arranging field trips a question as to whether any of the children will require unusual services. "Mainstreamed" pupils may have the full range of handicaps, including limited mobility, vision, or hearing. Some may have learning disabilities or other mental or emotional disturbances. Since some schools use field trips as an opportunity for integrating pupils in special classes with the rest of the school community, those that are disabled may not be regular members of the groups with which they appear. The organization's guide therefore needs to be aware that unusual situations may arise, so that preparations can be made to take them in stride.

Some historical societies have extended their educational endeavors in outreach programs to take society resources to various community groups in the groups' own locations. Such programs include traveling exhibits at banks, shopping centers, and malls. Traveling exhibits may also be installed in senior citizens' centers, nursing homes, and residential facilities for the severely disabled. Historical organization staff members who already take audiovisual presentations and sample artifacts to public school classes have found that handicapped groups and the elderly also enjoy such presentations, appropriately adapted for an audience of adults rather than children. One society director observed that, on such occasions, he had learned at least as much from older residents, who had, in youth, been familiar with objects similar to those in his collection, as they had learned from him. Another society has conducted a successful local history course in a nursing home and is training elderly citizens who are not disabled to offer the course in other nursing-care facilities. Memories of some nursing home residents could also add much to oral history collections. Made an activity of the junior historical organization, such a project could serve several purposes at once.

Accommodation for the disabled is important also to societies active in historic preservation in their communities. Reconciliation between accessibility and historical integrity is especially difficult in buildings being preserved for adaptive use. The conflicting requirements of building codes, preservation legislation, and the guidelines of funding agencies can create quite complex dilemmas, such as—for one example—the steep entrance steps, narrow doors, narrow hallways, and cramped staircases of row houses in urban districts. The National Trust position that "buildings are preserved for people" recognizes that inconspicuous modifications for improving accessibility become part of the continuing tradition of houses that have already been repeatedly altered by successive generations of historic occupants; but there is much more thinking to be done on this subject, and a concerned historical organization can well take the lead in its own community.

Accessibility considerations in a program of site marking arise principally from visual limitations. Markers should be placed at or near eye-level in locations where it is possible to stop a car to read them. Those of cast metal with raised or incised lettering can be helpful to blind people if they are put in locations where one may safely get out of the car to touch the marker's lettering. Painted lettering should be bold, simple, sharply contrasted with its background, and well protected from the weather. Brief texts are best, since most people will not want to read the whole history of the event commemorated;

and those who do can obtain brochures available at society headquarters. A line drawing, diagram, or map can truly be worth a thousand words, but photographs cannot be seen effectively from a distance.

"I Need Some Feedback"

When museum and historical society 504 co-ordinators have examined their programs, made simple and obvious adjustments, and are planning more elaborate adaptations, they will want to consult local disabled individuals and organizations in order, as one survey respondent observed, to prevent expenditure of limited time, energy, and resources on accommodations not likely to be used. Such consultations are mandated by the Section 504 guidelines, partly for that reason and partly because disabled persons are the best judges of their own interests and know a great deal about the obstacles that confront them and how such obstacles may be overcome. It is well to start by acquiring basic information about the disabled population of the area. Although census data is as yet of little help, the office of Advocate for the Handicapped now established in most states can provide some general information. Local agencies serving people with specific disabilities can tell most about the population the historical organization will actually serve. Directories of such agencies are often available from state or county offices of human resources.

The co-ordinator may well wish to start with a telephone survey of agencies listed in these directories, to identify those interested in co-operative activities. Some agencies concentrate on fund-raising and medical treatment, but many have recreation programs for which historical organization resources might be appropriate. Branches of nationwide groups, such as the Easter Seal Society and the March of Dimes, whose names are familiar from annual campaigns, vary so greatly that only inquiry will reveal their local circumstances. Other organizations may be agencies of state or local governments, which have a different point of view from private organizations. Schools, mental and rehabilitation hospitals, and nursing homes should also be included, as well as organizations of handicapped persons. The last, however, may be very small, and they are not always listed in a directory, so they may have to be reached by other means.

These agencies can introduce the historical society to the people each serves and to their constituents' disabilities. They will know much about needed equipment and services and where to procure them. They may know of sources of funds that will provide an additional cultural resource for their clients. Their members can put the historical organization in touch with the formal and informal communications network and with the structure of personal and political relationships through which disabled people get things done in their community. The organization may wish to start by working with one or two agencies in which members of its staff, board of directors, or volunteers have personal contacts. Persons with inside knowledge of both organizations can do a great deal to make initial joint activities, such as a museum tour for a group of children with cerebral palsy, run smoothly.

The co-ordinator may discover that many of these agencies are so deeply involved with their own work that they know little about the historical society. Disabled individuals, furthermore, may be unfamiliar with the historical society because they are unaccustomed to participating in cultural activities of any sort. It may be worthwhile, therefore, to prepare a brief presentation explaining the history and purpose of the historical organization, the results of the co-ordinator's assessment of its program, and its interest in welcoming the disabled part of the community. Such a talk should be limited to fifteen minutes, and can often be effectively illustrated with slides of the organization's accomplishments. It can be used to introduce the organization to service clubs and also to participants in its outreach program. Or a local television station might prepare a videotape that could also be featured on one of its public-service broadcasts.

The co-ordinator is then in a position to begin forming the advisory committee suggested in the guidelines. It is recommended that this body include persons familiar with the full range of disabilities—limited mobility, vision, hearing, mental capacity, and problems of older people. The committee should include both agency personnel and handicapped individuals, and their widely diverse social and educational backgrounds ought to be represented. The co-ordinator will of course be the chairman, and interested staff, board members, and volunteers may wish to attend selected meetings. Meetings will need to be held in an accessible location, and communication assistance should be provided for participants with limited vision or hearing. It may also be necessary to assist disabled persons in finding transportation, especially in the evening, when people who work will be free.

Although a fully representative advisory committee may be appropriate for a large state or regional historical society, smaller local organizations may find a group of large size unwieldy and overwhelming. It is, furthermore, burdensome for agency personnel with many other responsibilities and handicapped individuals with difficulty in getting from place to place to ask that they serve on a separate committee for every community agency required by the Section 504 guidelines to have one. It may therefore be more appropriate for the full advisory committee to be sponsored by a local or regional consortium of historical organizations and perhaps other cultural agencies. The co-ordinators of participating societies might attend, say, quarterly meetings of this group, to secure ideas about the full range of disabilities and find out what the various organizations are doing. They could then make contact, perhaps through members of the advisory committee, with members of local agencies prepared to assist them with specific activities.

One of these activities is review of the needs-assessment survey and completion of the "self-evaluation" form, for which such consultation is required by the guidelines. For this purpose it will be necessary for disabled representatives to tour the organization's facilities and perhaps attend some of its events. They can suggest local resources for overcoming obstacles, including sources of equipment, services, and funds. Then they can recommend various alternative methods for improving program accessibility. Determining the probable cost of these various proposals is a matter for staff research as much as committee discussion, but the co-ordinator may not be familiar with the sources of needed information. Committee members may therefore have to ask personnel from their own agencies to seek it out.

The self-evaluation will then describe each of the historical society's programs, indicating how handicapped persons can participate in each and what modifications are necessary to make that possible. It will analyze each of the organization's buildings, indicating obstacles to access and to public amenities such as rest rooms, water fountains, and telephones. It must describe employment practices, including advertising and recruitment. It is also a good idea to establish grievance procedures for consumer complaints. The document recording the completed self-evaluation must be signed and dated by the co-ordinator and kept on file at the organization's offices for review by anyone who wishes to see it. It does not have to be sent to Washington unless requested by one of the federal funding agencies, all of which will be satisfied by the same statement. The deadline is six months after the issuance of each agency's set of guidelines, but program adaptations not requiring structural modifications must have been put into effect three months *before* that date.

The historical organization will learn much from these contacts about the great diversity of its handicapped audience. The needs of persons with various disabilities are so different that they often have little in common with each other. People with limited mobility require architectural accessibility, which is far less important to those with limited vision or hearing, whose needs for assistance in communication may not be shared by others. Persons with mental limitations often experience kinds of discrimination different from those encountered by persons with mobility or sensory impairments. It is often wiser, therefore, to work with representatives of one disability at a time in arranging details of accommodations particularly important to them; but it is necessary to take care that adjustments for the benefit of one group do not create additional hazards for another.

There are also great sociological differences within the handicapped population. It is easy to think first of those in institutions, who are most likely to visit historical sites or

At Trout Hall, Allentown, Pennsylvania, steps are bypassed by a ramp, of which a visitor observed, "If it was not part of the original house, it should have been."—*Courtesy Lehigh County (Pa.) Historical Society*

museums on group tours. These include schools for blind, deaf, and mentally retarded children, many of which are preparing their pupils to enter the larger world when they grow up. Adults may come from mental hospitals, rehabilitation centers, and residential facilities, which some of them have entered quite recently and where others have spent most of their lives. Nevertheless, all of them share an isolation from many experiences that most people take for granted.

As has already been mentioned, historical organizations may discover that the majority of their handicapped audience is over sixty-five years old. Some are in nursing homes, others meet at senior citizens' centers, and still others live with their children but find it difficult to go out. All of them have in common, besides their disabilities, the point of view of their generation. Many of them passed most of their lives before local history and museum visiting became widely enjoyed leisure activities. Those who are not members of the historical society already may be unfamiliar with it and uncertain what to expect. But they often respond eagerly to activities that help them to remember what life was like when they were young, and they can contribute much to society projects concerning that era.

Persons disabled in adulthood by illness, accident, or wartime injury may be more independent than most of the institutionalized and the elderly handicapped. Many of them live with their families and are employed on all levels, from sheltered workshops to professional capacities. They often regard their impairments as unfortunate inconveniences and are frequently very ingenious at devising alternative ways of accomplishing things that they want to do. Some of these people were historical society members before they became disabled and continue their interest afterwards. They know what to expect and can suggest many worthwhile adaptations. Those with business or professional standing will be particularly helpful as members of the advisory committee, because they have inside knowledge of both worlds.

Many of these independent disabled people have grown impatient with policies and regulations established for the dependent majority. Such individuals have founded organizations of disabled consumers and organized the handicapped civil rights movement. Some of them were disabled in the Viet Nam war, and their plight added to the groundswell of public opinion that prompted the passage of the Rehabilitation Act of 1973 and the implementation of Section 504. These activists include some militants, who want the law that they have secured enforced strictly and all discrimination ended as soon as possible. Some of them who have spent their lives as shut-ins want to experience everything they have missed in the world. They often have misconceptions of the practical difficulties in the way and little knowledge of what must be done to overcome them.

Many museums and historical organizations, especially small ones, wonder how to deal with these militants without undertaking structural modifications far beyond their resources. It is best to meet these groups head-on, including their representatives on the advisory committee and giving their opinions full and fair hearing. Those individuals who want to do more can work on projects to put their ideas into practice, but the historical organization should make very clear to them the extent of its resources and its responsibility to maintain its total program. If the organization accepts the responsibility to include disabled people in its audience with good faith and good will, the vast majority of handicapped persons will respond in kind. Historical societies surveyed reported that, by and large, disabled people have been deeply appreciative of efforts made for their accommodation, such as the overwhelming response to a program of sign language tours that "flabbergasted" one society's board of directors.

Thus it becomes clear that museums and historical organizations can do much to include handicapped persons in their programs without undue trouble and expense. The requirements of the Section 504 guidelines that historical organizations define those programs, appoint someone to examine them, and invite disabled persons to contribute recommendations contain a great deal of common sense. As several survey respondents suggested, the very raising of many questions may point the way to solutions that can be accomplished by quite minor adjustments in policy or procedure.

Many historical societies have already gone further in that direction than they realize and can accomplish much by co-ordinating existing ad hoc adjustments into a coherent, consistent approach and then filling in the gaps. The society that works to know the handicapped part of its community and tackles the problem of accessibility with good faith and good will is not likely to become the target of a militant protest demonstration. Indeed, some societies may discover that many accommodations undertaken in the first instance for the benefit of disabled visitors actually improve service to the entire constituency.

3

"We Don't Have Any Special Programs"

EDUCATIONAL institutions, including museums, have for many years devised special programs for persons with various disabilities. Some of these programs have represented a great investment of time and material resources by professional experts in special education, and they have been directed either to the complex needs of the severely handicapped or to the mass audience of major museums. Particularly noteworthy have been several tactile galleries for the instruction and enjoyment of the blind, such as the museum of the Perkins Institute in Boston, the Mary Duke Biddle Gallery of the North Carolina Museum of Art, and the Lions Gallery of the Senses at the Wadsworth Atheneum in Connecticut. Yet, blind persons themselves have objected to these galleries, from some of which sighted persons were originally excluded, as tending to promote segregation of the blind from the whole museum world. The American Federation of the Blind has actually taken an official position against them, recommending instead that tactile exhibits be arranged for the general public. The Section 504 guidelines do not forbid such programs, but recommend by preference that disabled persons be accommodated in the most integrated setting consonant with their special needs.

Historical organizations, by and large, have not developed special programs for handicapped persons. Most of them are too small and receive too few disabled visitors. Nor are their staff members or volunteer guides trained in special education; so the handicapped groups that visit them, mostly school field trips, receive the usual tour with a few adjustments made on the spot. As one society responded to the survey, "We don't have any special programs." As a result, these historical societies are actually closer to the intention of Section 504 than are organizations with more elaborate special programs.

47

"We Are Doing Our Utmost to Have as Few Inaccessible Areas as Possible"

Many historical societies are facing the problem of providing access for persons with limited mobility to the buildings in which their activities take place. New or renovated structures must comply with building codes that require level entrances, elevators, and appropriate rest rooms in their original plans. Older buildings, however, often have entrance steps, steep and slippery stairs, and very inconvenient toilet facilities. When these buildings are historic structures, substantial alterations may be forbidden by the historic preservation regulations, or in many instances, they may be totally impracticable. Sometimes activities can be rescheduled elsewhere, but when that is impossible—as with guided tours of historic houses—structural modifications may be unavoidable. With some thought and planning, however, such modifications may prove to be much less extensive than originally anticipated.

The Section 504 guidelines allow three years for the completion of necessary alterations, but require the preparation of a "transition plan" explaining how such alterations are to be accomplished. The transition plan should be drawn up by the co-ordinator in co-operation with the advisory committee, after the completion of the self-evaluation. The plan must include a statement of the obstacles to be overcome, methods proposed for doing so, and a timetable of the steps to be accomplished each year until 1982. Like the completed self-evaluation, the transition plan too must be signed and dated by the co-ordinator and kept on file at the organization office for anyone who wishes to see it. Since it commits the organization to capital expenditures and perhaps to a major fund-raising effort, the board of directors will clearly play a crucial part in its planning as well as its execution. But there are many ways in which this requirement can be used to good purpose in making possible far-reaching improvements in the organization's facilities.

The difference between "barrier-free" and "accessible" structures has already been mentioned, and also the fact that the latter approach is acceptable under the Section 504 guidelines. After the passage of the Architectural Barriers Act of 1968, the American National Standards Institute (ANSI) developed specifications for accessible ramps, elevators, stairs, doors and hallways, rest rooms, water fountains, and public telephones. These specifications meet federal standards and have been incorporated in most state and local building codes. Some historic houses may have difficulty in complying with the codes for public buildings because they were built as private homes, for which the standards are much less strict. Some of these codes have no stated exceptions for historic structures like the regulations of the Department of the Interior, but it may be possible to obtain waivers on a case-by-case basis. Lawyers and architects on the board of directors of museums and historical organizations will be able to suggest ways to deal with state and local regulations. Advice can also be requested from the appropriate regional field office of the National Trust for Historic Preservation, 1785 Massachusetts Avenue N.W., Washington, D.C. 20036.

Many historical societies, especially larger ones, have their headquarters, library, and museum in fairly modern buildings with many accessible features. Some older headquarters buildings contain elevators, although they also often have entrance steps. Some are in historic public buildings, such as former courthouses, which are also used by other community agencies required to comply with Section 504. One survey respondent is housed in a former county hospital that is already completely accessible. Libraries and open-gallery museums often have wide doorways, smooth floors, and elevators. Some societies whose headquarters house basement or second-floor museums are developing outreach programs for persons who cannot reach these exhibit areas.

Many historic buildings have entrance steps, first floors that can be seen from a wheelchair, and second stories out of reach by reason of a staircase. Interior spaces may be cramped, and the structure may be incapable of bearing the weight of an elevator, but there are many opportunities for alternative interpretation. Some of these sites and most museum villages, have the additional problem of distance and uneven walk surfaces. Parks and historic sites must meet the needs of handicapped visitors while preserving their natural as well as their historic environment. Most recently built visitor centers meet the standards for accessibility, but those in older buildings do so only partially. For the most part, larger societies and those associated with the National Park Service or with state historical associations understand what is expected of them better than smaller, more localized organizations. Full-time directors are better informed than part-time volunteer curators or caretakers without professional training.

Although problems of accessibility are usually considered with reference to the 500,000 Americans who use wheelchairs, it is also important to remember the much larger number who use canes or crutches or are subject to easy exhaustion. Visitors in wheelchairs need smooth surfaces, cannot climb steps, and require ample room to turn and maneuver. Persons on crutches need nonskid surfaces, reasonably short distances to cover, and stairs with steps wide enough for effective balance. Those with uncertain balance or those likely to become easily exhausted, including many elderly persons, need, in addition, well-lighted

Entrance ramp at the new Exhibit Center, Macon County, Illinois, Museum Complex.—*Courtesy Macon County (Ill.) Historical Society*

stairways with sturdy handrails and ample opportunities to sit down. All these types of visitors and some others, as well, may have limited use of their hands, making it difficult for them to turn door handles or operate switches on self-service audiovisual equipment. Such needs must be taken into consideration together, so that modifications for the benefit of one group do not create additional hazards for another.

In order to be used by persons in wheelchairs, entrance steps must be replaced by a ramp. It has already been mentioned that the entrance most suitable for the purpose is the one with the fewest steps. If there are only one or two entrance steps, they can often be eliminated by regrading the walk, which can be gently sloped to blend with the surrounding ground on the sides as well as the approaching surface. The director of a historic house points out that the foundations for such a walk can be laid over historic steps without damaging

A regraded walkway provides access to the Schuyler Mansion in Albany, New York, without damaging the mansion's historic doorway.—*Photograph by Debbie Snook*

Portable ramp at the Frank Buchman House, Allentown, Pennsylvania, is stored in an unused coal hole under the porch and put in place when needed.—*Courtesy Lehigh County (Pa.) Historical Society*

them. He also suggests that such construction offers an excellent opportunity for an archaeological dig.

Temporary ramps, which can be put away when not needed, may offer a solution to historic houses that are open seasonally and have few visitors, but if there is frequent demand, they may impose a burden on maintenance personnel, as well as presenting some hazards to users unless they are firmly secured. Local volunteers can build these devices inexpensively of wood, metal, or other strong, lightweight materials. Such a ramp should rise no more steeply than one inch in one foot. A nonskid surface is essential for the safety of users of both wheelchairs and crutches. Portable ramps are also useful where there is a hazard to others, as at historic town houses with one or two steps to a busy sidewalk. At one such house, an ingenious collapsible ramp was designed that could be stored away in an abandoned coal hole when not in use. In such instances, that institution can properly request advance notice for special services when mentioning this feature in its brochure.

At historic houses with several steps at all entrances, a ramp of the required length—often forty or fifty feet—would be prohibitively expensive, as well as unsightly and unhistorical. Several historical societies with this problem are exploring the possibility of electric or hydraulic lifts. Some of these mechanisms can be installed unobtrusively on the steps at a side or rear entrance. There are also on the market inexpensive hydraulic lifts which, placed beside the steps, could raise a wheelchair to the height of the stoop. The mechanism is entirely underground, and the platform would sink to ground level when not in use and could be concealed by some very minor landscaping. Either of these lifts could be installed at a side or rear entrance where they would not interfere with the historical and architectural integrity of the front portico.

Touring the second story of historical buildings presents a number of problems. Headquarters, libraries, and museums housed in fairly modern structures usually have stairways conforming to the ANSI standards for public buildings. Persons on crutches need steps not more than six or eight inches high and at least four feet wide, with treads nine inches wide,

Wheelchair lift installed at the Kearney Mansion Museum in Fresno, California. Lift sinks out of sight when not in use. Here, it is shown just after use, with the platform raised to porch-floor level and the gate open.— *Courtesy Fresno City and County (Cal.) Historical Society*

to balance securely. The ANSI standards for handrails specify height from the floor, distance from the wall, and circumference, and require that they extend a foot and a half beyond the top and bottom of each flight. In a few large museums with mass audiences, escalators may provide rapid transit for some persons with limited mobility, but are hazardous for anyone with uncertain balance and cannot be used by people in wheelchairs.

Some historic mansions have wide and gracious staircases, though cramped landings are characteristic of eighteenth-century architecture. The homes of more ordinary early settlers often contain steep and hazardous flights crowded into very small areas to conserve heat and save space. The steps are frequently wedge-shaped and of uneven height, and there are no handrails. Such stairs are dangerous for

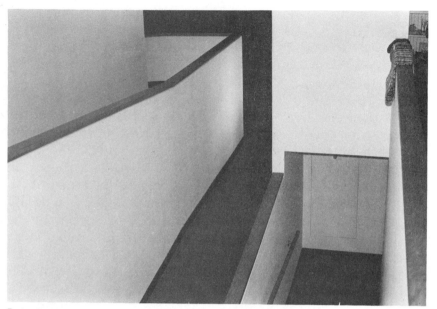

Interior ramps at new Exhibit Center, Macon County, Illinois, Museum Complex.—*Courtesy Macon County (Ill.) Historical Society*

anyone, and persons with limited mobility are well advised to avoid them. Steps without risers create apprehension in blind people who depend on the risers to assure them that their feet are placed where they will not trip. All stairs should be well lighted so that persons with impaired vision or uncertain balance can be sure of where they are going.

Historical societies with modern headquarters or those housed in buildings shared with other public agencies often have elevators that comply with ANSI standards. Some historic houses also have elevators, installed by their historic occupants, perhaps as a trunk-lift or mechanical dumbwaiter, or occasionally for use by a disabled resident. These elevators may be very small, so that some persons in wheelchairs cannot use them, but they may be very helpful to those who use canes or crutches, or those who have heart or lung conditions that prevent them from climbing stairs. Nor is the installation of an elevator necessarily inconsistent with preserving the architectural integrity of a historic house. At one such house, an appropriate location was found in two closets, placed one over the other, in a nineteenth-century stair well, although an architectural survey later revealed that the structure of the house could not carry the additional weight. Another possibility that deserves further exploration is stair lifts, some of which are unobtrusive enough to be used in historic buildings with straight, well-braced staircases. If the historic construction and materials would be damaged by either of these alternatives, however, that fact needs to be clearly explained to disabled individuals and groups, who may not be aware of it.

If the historical society headquarters is lodged in a public building, especially one also used by other agencies, rest rooms must comply with the ANSI accessibility standards. These standards require in essence that one rest room for each sex on each floor be equipped with level doors wide enough for wheelchairs, one stall wide enough for a person to transfer sideways from a wheelchair to the toilet, and grab bars to assist in sitting and rising. If the historical society does not receive large numbers of visitors with limited mobility, it may be sufficient for its purposes if there is one of these facilities for each sex somewhere in the building. But it should be pointed out that some toilets complying with existing ANSI standards cannot in fact be used by many persons in wheelchairs. The author observed one—not at a historical society building or a museum—that would require a user to stand up, turn completely around, and maneuver clothing out of the way before sitting down, and there was no room to close the door! These standards are now being revised, but historical organizations would be well advised to insist that their architects ask disabled persons which public toilets in the community are most convenient for them before installing new ones.

Many historic houses do not provide rest room facilities for any visitors, most of whom come only for brief tours. Some may wish to designate for handicapped visitors a single unisex toilet that can also serve employees. That arrangement reduces expense, prevents unnecessary duplication of facilities that may be infrequently used, and may be more consonant with existing plumbing. It also meets the needs, not envisioned by the building code, of disabled persons requiring assistance from relatives of the opposite sex. All such facilities must be clearly marked with the international accessibility symbol. It is also important that these rest rooms be kept unlocked and that door fasteners on the inside be very easy to operate for persons with limited use of their hands.

Historical societies that operate several historic buildings or a museum village must give special attention to walk surfaces and distances. Persons with limited mobility need walk surfaces at least four feet wide, with a hard, smooth surface in good repair. Administrators of some historic sites, believing that asphalt or concrete sidewalks are out of keeping with the site's authenticity, insist on gravel paths—difficult for anyone with trouble walking and impossible for those in wheelchairs. Flagstones or bricks are an acceptable alternative if they are firmly, closely set and provide a level surface, but stepping stones can be hazardous. One major museum is experimenting

Access ramp enters the back door of 1860s log house at the Prairie Village of the Macon County, Illinois, Museum Complex, Decatur, Illinois.—*Courtesy Macon County (Ill.) Historical Society*

with an oil base covered with gravel close-packed with a steam roller, which it is hoped will be smooth enough for wheelchairs as well as water-repellent. One museum village uses a very attractive conglomerate of pebbles bonded with cement that could well be more widely adopted. If suitable walk surfaces cannot be provided, it may be necessary to permit disabled visitors to approach the entrance in their cars.

Particularly at museum villages, it might be worthwhile to consider using a small vehicle with a self-contained ramp to overcome the triple problems of distance, uneven ground, and access to individual buildings with one or two steps. There are on the market some such vehicles for the outdoor transportation of wheelchairs, and some larger historical organizations might consider investing in one. Or it would be possible to adapt for two or three wheelchairs a boat or snowmobile trailer with a low axle, a level platform, and a side-mounted ramp of the type used in wheelchair vans. If such a ramp were let down over the steps, wheelchair users could be discharged directly into the historic building. The trailer could be pulled by any small vehicle the institution owns for security or other purposes. The expense of such adaptations would have to be met by outside funding, but it is to be hoped that some organizations will experiment with it. Audiovisual interpretation in the visitor center, however well done, is not an adequate substitute for the village experience.

"We Are Working to Increase the Scope of Our Communication"

As the historical organization examines its program, it may discover ways in which communication with some disabled people can be improved by various mechanical adaptations. Visitors with limited mobility who cannot reach areas such as the second stories of historic houses may share in the tour experience by alternative interpretation. Those with limited vision will appreciate tactile maps and models and labels and literature in Braille, large type, or cassette recordings. Library materials and publications can be made available through recording services and radio stations for the blind.

Individuals with impaired hearing will appreciate appropriate printed materials and perhaps electronic amplification, as well as sign-language interpreters. All these adaptations should be planned and carried out in close co-operation with members of the advisory committee and others fully familiar with the techniques concerned, who will be able to make many valuable suggestions.

One way to present the story of a historic building's second floor to those who must remain downstairs is through a series of large color photographs, including interiors of each room and close-ups of selected objects. The disabled visitor could then examine these pictures while the guide presents the usual interpretation of the second story, or taped cassettes could be provided, which would permit the guide to take the rest of the party upstairs at the same time. Much can also be added to this approach by bringing down a few featured objects, so that the disabled visitor can appreciate their color, texture, and weight. That procedure can also help the visitor to overcome the distortion of perspective inevitable in two-dimensional representations of three-dimensional objects. This technique has been effectively used for a group of children from a heart hospital visiting a historic house where, as often happens, toys are displayed in a second-floor children's bedroom. The method may be particularly appropriate for small historic sites with no professional staff and few visitors.

Another method is a slide set, kept with its projector on a small rolling table to be used wherever convenient. Individual wheelchair visitors can use a rear-screen projector in a very small space, while, for disabled groups, the slides can be projected on any light-colored wall. Showing them in one of the historic rooms not only maintains an appropriate atmosphere, but permits visitors to imagine the second story in the context of their observations of the first. This presentation should not take more than the fifteen minutes most visitors spend on the second floor. That means featuring about thirty slides, since the human eye takes about a half-minute to see and appreciate each image. The set should include general interior views, to show the arrangement of each room; close-ups of selected significant objects; and a few particularly interesting details.

Additional slides may also be available if visitors are interested in objects mentioned but not featured. A volunteer may have the equipment and expertise to take pictures of suitable quality, or students in a local school of photography could be invited to make it a class project.

These slides may be shown by the guide, who will give the usual presentation, allowing visitors ample opportunity to ask questions about things in which they are particularly interested. Or a tape cassette with an automatic slide-changing mechanism can be provided, to permit the disabled visitor to view the set while the guide takes the main tour group upstairs, so that no portion of the party has to wait for the other. Scripts so used should allow about one hundred words per minute, or fifty per slide, and may tell a story about the people who used these rooms and the activities they carried on there. Individual objects are most interesting to handicapped visitors, as to visitors in general, as things that people made and used, rather than as examples of particular decorative styles. A

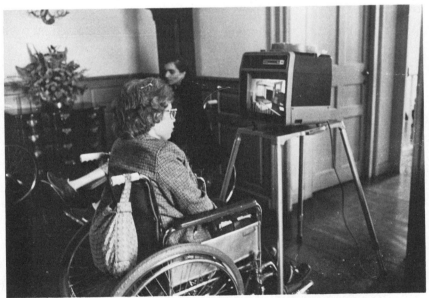

Disabled visitor views a slide interpretation of the second story of the Schuyler Mansion at Albany, New York.—*Photograph by Debbie Snook*

printed version of this script may be made available for use by the deaf.

Videotape has also been suggested as an appropriate means of alternative interpretation. One historical society that made such a tape happened to have a director with experience in professional television, a volunteer with the necessary equipment and expertise, and a guide who was a semiprofessional performing artist. Filming was therefore completed without undue trouble and expense, and a grant for purchase of projection equipment was secured from a local foundation. This videotape has been well received by disabled visitors and museum professionals. It achieves the immediacy of an actual tour by costumed guides, complete with demonstrations, but slides may be more effective for close-ups of individual objects. A museum educator also points out that care must be taken in using videotape presentations to guard

Filming the videotape of the second story of Trout Hall, Allentown, Pennsylvania.—*Photograph by Andrew Moore*

against the passive receptivity many people find habitual when viewing television.

Persons with limited vision may find maps or models helpful in locating the areas of large historical museums that they wish to visit. If there is a floor plan at the entrance, it needs to be simply drawn with bold, black lettering and hung in a good light. Some blind visitors may find a three-dimensional model of historic buildings helpful. Such a model should be mounted horizontally rather than vertically, and positioned in the direction the visitor is facing. One site plans not merely a model of the exterior of its historic house, but one of the surrounding neighborhood, and another of the interior of a single room. Such models, which must be done to scale to be effective, have so far been produced by professional firms, but it is possible that historical society volunteers interested in the construction and collection of miniature furniture might be able to prepare one.

Although some blind individuals and organizations object strongly to tactile galleries designed exclusively for them, they

Three-dimensional model of Independence Mall Historic Site is helpful to blind visitors.—*Courtesy National Park Service. Photograph by Marti Degen*

eagerly encourage tactile exhibits available for all visitors. Some art museums have designed exhibits of this type around such concepts as texture or shape, and both blind and sighted artists have produced works specifically for that purpose. Most history museums, especially historic houses, contain many objects that visitors in general might handle to appreciate texture and weight and to perceive the strength needed to operate their moving parts. A kitchen or workshop might be designated for this purpose, since such things would often normally be kept there. There may also be displays in other rooms, if the distinction between what may and may not be touched is clearly stated. That would add an important dimension to the interpretation of historic buildings, whose contents, after all, were made not to be looked at with awe, but to be used by people not so different from ourselves.

Where a historical organization does not provide guided tours of its museums, many blind visitors prefer cassette recordings to other means of information. Some major museums will lend or rent to all visitors recorded commentaries—some of which run an hour or longer—on temporary or permanent exhibitions. Most historical museum visitors, however, do not want that much information. One historical society that has received a grant to prepare such recordings recommends that they not exceed two to four minutes for each room. That will include a brief description of the room's general significance and the contents of the labels on various objects. Playback equipment is inexpensive, and earplugs will permit visitors to hear without disturbing others.

A historical society may also wish to tape brochures or other literature and offer them alongside printed versions on sale in the gift shop. Since such recordings can often be made at little cost by the museum's volunteers or by those in libraries for the blind, it is possible to charge the same price as for print versions, which many blind persons prefer to receiving them free. The regional library for the blind can be of great assistance, particularly in recommending the most appropriate equipment for preparing recordings that blind persons can play on the machines issued to them by various reading services. Such libraries may also be interested in recording for their collections significant materials from the historical society archives. In some states, indeed, the state library for the blind has projects for recording regional materials that have placed considerable emphasis on items of local history. Volunteers from one historical society and a library for the blind work together in preparing local history materials to be read over the air on a nearby radio station for the blind; copies of these tapes are then lodged in the historical society library.

Persons with limited vision can often read posters that have bold and black lettering, do not contain too much information, and are hung at or slightly above eye level in a good light. The preparation of exhibit labels and brochures in large type has already been mentioned. When preparing materials for such reproduction, it is well to remember that people who use them often read slowly and with great difficulty. They appreciate brief presentations with short sentences and paragraphs and carefully selected details. For those who skim, the subject of each paragraph needs to be clear from the first few words. Society publications can be reproduced in such a format without additional typesetting—though on somewhat larger pages—by a magnification process in offset printing.

Since there are only about 40,000 persons fluent in Braille in the entire United States, and they are very unevenly distributed, the historical society should consult local associations for and of the blind to determine whether there is likely to be a demand for materials in Braille. If so, these agencies will have the equipment and expertise to assist in producing experimental Braille labels and brochures. For a historic house, the text of such a brochure could well fit into one page, with a second page providing raised line drawings of the facade of the house and floor plans of the first and second stories. Text and drawings can be inexpensively reproduced by a process known as "thermoform," for which the blind association will again have access to equipment. Outdoor labels at historic sites may contain both large-type and Braille texts and should be waterproof. Some national parks, however, have observed that, for some reason, such Braille labels are peculiarly subject to vandalism.

There are various forms of electronic amplification that

persons with impaired hearing can use to supplement their own hearing aids. One national park has a system that a visitor may plug in to assist in hearing the narration accompanying its electronic map recapitulation of the events of the battle fought there. A survey respondent has audio tapes explaining a set of dioramas that a visitor with limited hearing may turn up to additional volume. It is also possible to install at certain seats in the auditorium individual listening devices similar to those used in some churches. A general public address system may be helpful in lecture halls if the person operating it is sufficiently familiar with the equipment to be able to eliminate echoes and confusing distortions. It is important to remember that background noise can create distracting "feedback" on hearing aids, so that visitors using them may have great difficulty in crowded and noisy situations.

Deaf persons can enjoy captioned audiovisual presentations. Inserting captions on slides requires some complicated photographic processes, but separate slides containing explanatory text can be prepared inexpensively. Items can be spelled out on a flannelgraph or with plastic letters on a peg board—black on white or white on black—and photographed with an ordinary camera. The ideal way to show these slides is by double projection, with the picture on one screen and the text on the other. If two projectors are not available, however, the text slides can be inserted before the picture they describe—or before a sequence of two or three. In projecting such sets, it is important to allow sufficient time for deaf viewers to read the text as well as appreciate the pictures.

Several workers with the deaf recommend appropriate printed materials as the most practicable way for small historical organizations to communicate with occasional deaf visitors. Most societies surveyed that reported such materials available turned out, upon inquiry, to use for that purpose the materials distributed to the general public. But these may not be appropriate, since deafness cuts a person off from language as well as sound, and many deaf people are not well educated, especially if they have been deaf from birth. They therefore need concrete words and short, simple sentences; they may find complex grammatical constructions such as split infinitives and the passive voice particularly confusing. Since their education often includes little instruction in history, they may be unfamiliar with much background information and many events that most visitors take for granted.

A deaf person's guide to a historic home might begin with a few sentences setting the house and its occupants in their general historical period. A few more sentences might then describe the contents of each room with reference to the activities that the householders performed there. These guides should be written as stories about people doing things, rather than as a description of objects. Many of the deaf may be unsure of the vocabulary and the differences between such decorative styles as Queen Anne and Chippendale, so such descriptive terms, if used, should be illustrated. If these printed guides for the deaf are typed on a typewriter with large type and reproduced by offset printing, each page can contain a description of a room and a picture. It is important to remember that deaf people think in pictures, so that, for them, the illustrations explain the text rather than the other way around.

It is essential that all equipment used to improve communication be sturdy, easy to operate, and in good repair, to avoid mechanical failures disappointing to visitors—handicapped or not—and embarrassing to society staff members and volunteers. Instructions for self-service equipment need to be written simply and clearly, perhaps color-coded with switches, and posted where visitors cannot miss them. Those in charge of lending cassette players to blind visitors should make sure that the borrowers understand how to use all necessary equipment. Personnel responsible for showing slides, videotapes, and films need plenty of practice in setting up and running the projectors and in dealing with such minor emergencies as jammed slides, for which the necessary tools and a supply of spare parts, including batteries and fuses, should always be within easy reach. Rented films should always be previewed as soon as they arrive, and defective copies should be reported to the supplier, while materials in frequent use need to be reviewed regularly for indications of wear. It is important to establish a working relationship with a reliable, prompt, and efficient repair service, perhaps through a board member or a volunteer who has some connection with such a business. Such precautions can vastly reduce the instances when carefully prepared presentations are disrupted or spoiled altogether by mechanical malfunctions.

"The Basic Premise Is 'Don't Hover' "

A number of survey respondents emphasize that training staff members and volunteers to meet the needs of disabled visitors is at least as important as any architectural or mechanical modification. The organization's personnel may need instruction in the use of such equipment as rear-screen slide projectors, videotape players, and cassette recorders. They should know suitable techniques for communicating with people whose vision, hearing, and mental capacity is limited. They should also know something about the nature of various disabilities and the ways in which such impairments may affect visitors. Some needed instruction may take place at meetings led by personnel from local agencies and by disabled individuals. Staff members may also wish to attend workshops and conferences sponsored by regional consortia or national organizations such as the American Association for State and Local History.

A series of meetings on the various types of disabilities could well be part of a year's program for the guides' guild. A museum educator who has conducted such meetings observes that they ought to be compulsory, since all guides can expect to encounter handicapped visitors at some time. Each meeting can be limited to a particular type of disability, and agency personnel or disabled individuals would be useful participants. A meeting could begin with a lecture or film to provide basic information. There should be ample time for discussion, including expression of feelings of anger, shyness, or embarrassment in the presence of handicapped people. Consideration of future plans could follow, with identification of members who would like to help with them.

Simulating the experience of handicapped persons can be an extremely helpful part of such meetings, if participants keep in mind that this is merely an introduction to the problem and cannot provide adequate understanding of what it means to live with it. When guides take turns sitting in the institution's wheelchair and pushing each other through the first floor of a historic house, they see the collection from the angle of vision of a seated person. They also experience that it may be difficult to hear while sitting several inches below the level at which sound normally travels from one standing adult to another. Those pushing the wheelchair can observe the amount of time and space needed to maneuver the chair into the best position for viewing a room, and can establish more clearly where these locations are, giving the staff people some idea how to modify their own presentations for people sitting there. This experience will also make it clear that the person pushing the wheelchair should not, as a rule, also be responsible for interpreting the room, since it is awkward to do an interpretation from behind the visitor. The staff can further note obstacles and perhaps suggest some minor readjustments in the positioning of furniture.

Staff members and volunteers also need to be informed of

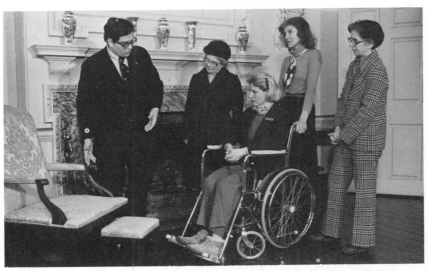

Guides at Cliveden, in Philadelphia, learn to appreciate the point of view of disabled visitors by touring the museum in a wheelchair.—*Courtesy National Trust for Historic Preservation*

the organization's policies concerning the offering of assistance to disabled visitors. Some staff members are glad to push wheelchairs when asked, but others, including some elderly volunteers who may have disabilities of their own, would prefer to be excused. The administration should check with the organization's insurance carrier to determine the extent of liability coverage before allowing staff members to carry disabled persons up or down stairs. If staff people are to perform that service, they should receive appropriate training from rehabilitation personnel and be supplied with suitable equipment. Disabled persons being carried by their relatives or friends may be asked to sign waivers absolving the organization of liability, in case anyone should be injured on its premises. These dangers are important reasons why all historical organizations and museums should make every effort to provide access by other means.

Staff members and guides need to know that some persons with limited vision appreciate offers of assistance, while others prefer to ask for it when they need it. It may be necessary to attract the attention of a totally blind person by a touch on the *arm*—never touch a blind person's cane or guide dog—and by addressing him or her directly, identifying one's self, since the blind cannot see who is speaking to them. Persons who come with canes or guide dogs are accustomed to traveling alone and have many ways of finding directions for themselves. Since guide dogs are trained to avoid objects in their path, museums need not fear for their collections, though some have a limit on the number of dogs permitted in the building at one time. The best way to assist blind persons is to permit them to take one's arm and find their own way, rather than taking the blind visitor's arm and attempting to steer him. Since blind people are particularly afraid of tripping, they will want to be informed of abrupt changes in level, as well as overhanging objects and projecting pieces of furniture.

Although some blind visitors to a historical museum may experience the collection entirely by touch, 90 percent of the legally blind have some residual vision. They can see a great deal if staff members or guides will help them locate the objects to which they wish to direct their attention. On entering a room, the guide needs to help them orient themselves by describing the room's function and mentioning the principal objects it contains. It is particularly important to encourage them to ask questions about things they cannot see well. They can probably discover the size, shape, and texture of artifacts for themselves, but will need help with color, line, and fine details. They may appreciate the offer of a large magnifying glass for this purpose.

Totally blind persons have varying degrees of touch or visual orientation, depending on the age at which they lost their sight. Those who were born blind or became so in early childhood have usually been trained in the technique of touching in schools for the blind. Those who lost their sight as adults may understand much by referring to their memories of the visual world. Analogies may be very helpful in describing objects to them. One staff member described the exterior of a historic building as "like a castle, higher than the tallest trees." The interior was explained as "four tiers of balconies surrounding an open area and supported by four-sided pillars." A butter print to be passed from hand to hand is depicted as "a round disk with a doorknob-shaped handle and a carved wheat-sheaf design."

A group of blind visitors learned a great deal by touching the elaborate furnishings of a sumptuous Victorian mansion. The staff found it helpful in avoiding confusion to invite blind persons to touch a few significant pieces in each room. The blind readily perceived the difference in temperature between the simulated marble of the entrance hall walls and the real marble of a bust of George Washington. They delighted in the elaborate decoration of large pieces of furniture covered with richly carved flowers and foliage. The heavy embroidery of an antique bed covering and brocaded upholstery fabrics gave them great pleasure; and they enjoyed the texture and odor of old leather bindings on rare books in the family library.

Effective communication is particularly important for dealing with deaf visitors, for those who have never heard think in pictures, rather than in sequences of words, and they use English almost as a second language. Those accustomed to speech may be able to follow it by lip-reading or may require assistance from the written word. It is important to note that persons who cannot hear use vision, instead, to orient themselves, and when they cannot see, communication is lost. Since they can only look in one direction at once, they cannot see the object and printed, signed, or spoken interpretation at the same time. Guides should make it a practice to stand facing any group in a good light. They should look at the group while they are speaking and avoid turning to direct attention to the object until they have finished speaking.

A number of historical organizations surveyed report that they have instructed their guides to speak slowly and distinctly for persons who lip-read, but almost none have asked professional teachers of lip-reading or members of an association for the deaf to instruct them in doing so. As a result, some guides try too hard, and mouth the words or drag out sentences, which can be very confusing. Others shout, which distorts the sound, especially for persons using hearing aids. It is best to speak at a normal speed and normal tone of voice, and not think too much about it. Nevertheless, since only about one-third of any word appears on the lips, lip-reading is at best an educated guess. Guides should expect lip-readers to ask to have information repeated, sometimes more than once, and each guide should carry a pad and pencil to write down troublesome phrases when necessary.

Inability to hear implies no inability to speak, and deaf visitors may wish to ask questions. Those who have lost their hearing as adults will do so as anyone else does, though their voices may be a bit harsh. They will receive the answers by lip-reading, or they may ask to have them written down. Persons who have been taught to speak without hearing the sound of their own voices may be difficult to understand. Most of them visit museums or historic sites with relatives or friends to interpret for them, or the guide can ask them to write down what they want to know. If one member of a group of deaf people asks a question, the question should be repeated to the entire group and the answer directed to the group.

At present, most deaf people who use manual sign language visit historical societies and museums in groups from schools or other organizations, such as senior citizens' centers, who bring their own interpreters. Sign language has a visually oriented conceptual base completely independent of English grammar. Museum guides and interpreters therefore need to give some thought to working together, and they would profit by an opportunity to practice before a tour. It is important that the guide and the interpreter stand side by side, next to the exhibit being discussed, so that the deaf audience can look from one to the other without strain. The guide should speak reasonably slowly, in simple sentences, without undue detail. Tours should last no more than a half-hour, because if the interpreter is weary the gestures can lose their crispness and become confusing.

A teacher from a school for the deaf observes that sign language contains few expressions for technical terms and abstract concepts. Such expressions can be communicated by finger spelling, if absolutely necessary, but the technique is exhausting and the problem of translating too many technical or abstract ideas can be overwhelming. Instead, the teacher suggests that abstract ideas be explained in terms of concrete objects and actions. Historical society and museum staff members and volunteers are almost never skilled in sign language, and some workers with the deaf advise them against trying to learn this complex skill hastily, particularly since there are two systems of sign language that have little in common. Others believe that knowledge of a few simple signs, such as those for giving directions and the finger-spelling alphabet, can help to make deaf visitors feel welcome.

Some large museums are experimenting with sign language interpretation on videotape. One teacher of the deaf advises against that, observing that on most television screens the hands of the interpreter will be too small to be seen clearly. Besides, the television monitor must be kept at a fixed location, while the objects being described may be in different rooms. It is therefore impossible for the deaf visitor to look from one to the other in order to understand what is being described. The fixed pace of the television interpretation allows him no opportunity to take in information at his own speed or to ask questions. For the present, therefore, most historical societies can find more effective and less expensive ways of communicating with deaf visitors.

Accommodating persons with mental limitations is almost entirely a matter of understanding how to meet their special needs. Adjustments in staff procedure are very different from those required for persons with limited mobility or sensory perception. Visitors who are mentally limited may include patients from mental hospitals, children with emotional disturbances or learning disabilities, and mentally retarded citizens of all ages, as well as individuals recovering from alcoholism or drug abuse. At present, most of these people come from institutions in organized groups for recreational therapy. Some may arrive with family or friends or, in the case of learning-disabled children, as "mainstreamed" pupils in ordinary public school classes. Historical society and museum staff members and volunteers therefore need to be prepared to welcome them, either in groups for activities planned in advance with their teachers or supervising hospital personnel, or as individuals who walk in the door without notice.

Pesonnel from mental hospitals point out that their patients are included in groups to participate in community activities only when they have recovered from illness sufficiently to display few symptoms of it in public. It has been suggested that their principal difference from visitors in general is that most patients in state mental hospitals come from sociological backgrounds in which museum visiting is not a normal leisure activity. Museum staff members, however, would not always agree. One staff person finds mental patients unusually passive, either from the heavy sedation with which they are being treated, or from their long experience as patients permitted to make few if any decisions for themselves. Other museum personnel have encountered short attention spans and behavior problems in visitors who are mental patients, and point out that tours for such groups must be shorter and simpler than usual, and groups should be limited in size and supervised by at least one hospital staff member for every five patients. It can also be emphasized that Section 504 requires equal, not special, treatment, and that mental patients, like any other visitors, may be expelled if they persist in troublesome behavior.

The official definition of a learning-disabled child is one who, at school age, cannot read or write in a normal manner.

The most common reasons for that difficulty are dyslexia and similar conditions in which visual and auditory symbols become distorted as they enter the brain, so that objects as well as words are seen in other than normal positions—upside down, sideways, or without depth perception. Dyslectic persons also have a short attention span and great difficulty in putting items in sequence or bringing ideas together to form a coherent whole. Learning-disabled children need short, simple presentations that repeat key words. The teacher of such a group and the historical society or museum staff member might make a list of key words to be used in an interpretation beforehand, so that the teacher can introduce them in the classroom, and the staff member can be sure to use them. Many children with dyslexia cannot answer and are embarrassed by the inductive questions often used to encourage pupils to draw their own conclusions—to infer, for example, that a spinning wheel and loom seen in different rooms were both used in the production of cloth.

Historical society and museum visits for groups of learning-disabled children should be simply constructed around a single idea—say, "Food in Olden Times." There need to be opportunities to use as many of the senses as possible, particularly that of touch. Demonstrations are particularly effective, especially those in which the pupils can participate. Thus, in an Early American kitchen, they can watch the society staff member mix cooky dough from an old recipe—perhaps taking turns helping her stir it—and cut out cookies, themselves, with antique cooky-cutters. Then they can smell the cookies baking in the old wood stove, while they listen to the crackle of the fire, play with small kitchen utensils, and enjoy the taste of the goodies eaten hot from the pan when they are done. They can enter the spirit of the occasion even more if the staff member is in costume and there are old-time garments, such as three-cornered hats, fichus, and aprons, for the children themselves to put on.

In a simpler presentation on the same subject, the guide could ask the children to identify the shape of a cooky-cutter—say, a cat—and ask them to repeat the word *cat*. The guide could trace the shape of the cooky-cutter with one finger and mention that in olden times people liked to make cookies in the shapes of things that they knew. Then the group could be asked, "Do you have a cat at home? Would you like to make a cooky shaped like a cat?" and let the child trace the shape with his finger. Thus the child could associate a historic artifact with his own everyday experience. A short and simple story will also help learning-disabled children recognize the significance of an object.

These suggestions were contributed by a teacher of learning-disabled children and the mother of a dyslectic child. They pointed out that these children are no more likely to be hyperactive or emotionally disturbed than children in general, and they may be highly intelligent. In many states, learning-disabled children are "mainstreamed" in regular public school classes so that they will rarely visit historical sites or museums as a group. It is further estimated that between 5 percent and 20 percent of the population have some form of learning disability, most of which are undiagnosed. Fortunately, the adjustments such individuals need most—simple, story-centered presentations with ample opportunity to touch objects—will also improve communication with younger visitors in general.

Emotionally disturbed children are usually disabled by a lack of self-confidence, which causes them to ignore the common conventions of social behavior. Some such children may become withdrawn and inattentive; others have a short attention span and are easily distracted. Their visits to museums and historical sites need to be short and carefully planned, with ample opportunity for them to touch objects. The museum staff member meeting the group can help by making a point of learning and using each child's name, seeking out opportunities for praising each one individually, and being sensitive to their needs as small people who have much more right than wrong with them. So that each child can receive individual attention, the group should be divided into parties of not more than six pupils, each accompanied by a museum staff member and a volunteer or an aide from the school. Objects given to the children to touch should be sturdy and free from sharp points, so that they can be handled freely and safely; small kitchen utensils, for example, such as sturdy mugs or spoons, might be suitable.

Mentally retarded persons include the "educable," who

can learn basic conceptual skills such as the rudiments of reading and arithmetic, and the "trainable," who can learn simple mechanical tasks by imitating the actions of others. Persons from these two classifications comprise the vast majority of retarded citizens and those most likely to come to museums or historical sites. Some of them may have other disabilities, such as limited vision or hearing or poor co-ordination of speech or mobility, but the severely and profoundly retarded, who may have limited control of many bodily functions, are often unable to profit much from museum visits, so they are not usually brought there. Some retarded people who cannot manage the co-ordination for effective speech are quite capable of understanding what is said to them if the content and vocabulary are within their range of comprehension. Abstract ideas mean nothing to them, and they associate all new information with their own direct experience. Although their minds work in many ways like those of children, retarded adults are very much aware that they are adults and resent being patronized or talked down to. Because retarded people have little awareness of time beyond yesterday, today, and tomorrow, they have no sense of history, but they have good memories for pleasurable—and painful—experiences and will readily recognize objects that have impressed them before. Their visits should be brief and centered around a few items used by other people for familiar activities, such as eating, sleeping, and getting from place to place, with story-centered presentations focused upon everyday experience and many opportunities for participation and use of all the senses.

The mother of an eight-year-old trainable child who has visited several museums offers valuable insights into his response. To him, all words represent concrete objects, rather than abstract ideas. A painting of the Madonna and Child, for example, is, to him, a picture of a mother and a baby playing. He can recognize colors and identify one part of the picture as light and another as dark, but he has no awareness of aesthetic values. He can understand that this child's name is Jesus, as his brother's name is Gary, but he has no awareness that Jesus might be a very special person.

He associates all ideas and actions with his own experi-

Handicapped children learn to spin wool during "Craft Days" at Rocky Mount Historical Society, Piney Flats, Tennessee.—*Courtesy Rocky Mount (Tenn.) Historical Society*

ence and cannot comprehend another person's point of view except by comparing it with his own. He knows, for example, that when someone hits him, it hurts and makes him want to cry, so that he must not hit his brother because that would make *him* hurt and want to cry. His sense of time is limited to yesterday, today, and tomorrow, separated by the ritual of going to bed, sleeping, and getting up again. He cannot imagine his mother as a little girl, or any events in which he has not participated.

Personnel at museums and historic sites also need to give some thought to their own attitudes and those of handicapped people. Most staff members and volunteers sincerely want to help, but are often uncertain how best to do so. Quite unintentionally, they may give an impression of patronizing over-solicitude, which some disabled persons resent as a subtle form of reverse discrimination. That unfortunate misconception may be created by language, for, like members of other minorities, some handicapped individuals are very sensitive to words they consider damaging to their self-respect. Most of the expressions concerned have in common that they tend to create impressions that the persons they describe are helpless objects of charity, something less than responsible adult human beings.

One example is the word *handicap,* itself, which, in sports such as golf or horse racing, signifies the additional weight some competitors carry in order to equalize the odds. The *Oxford English Dictionary* tells us that the word *handicap* was derived from the name of a game, "hand in cap," mentioned in *Piers Plowman* and popular in the seventeenth century, in which players drew lots from a cap to indicate the disadvantage they would have to overcome. It was first applied to horse racing in the eighteenth century, and to disabled persons by Lillian Wald in *The House on Henry Street* (1915). There is also a bit of folklore that the word is derived from the "handy cap," or workman's headgear, in which English laborers disabled by accidents of the early Industrial Revolution collected the bounty flung to street beggars by passers-by. Most people believe that its application to disabled persons signifies the additional burden they have to bear. These individuals, however, often believe that being called "handicapped" directs attention to their limitations, rather than their accomplishments.

Some people therefore prefer the word *disabled,* but others object that it too draws attention to their incapacities, rather than their capacities. A useful distinction might be drawn by using *disabled* to denote persons who have incurred an impairment as adults, after having learned to function in the world, while reserving *handicapped* for those who were born with their limitation or acquired it in early childhood. At present, however, the two words are usually regarded as interchangeable synonyms.

A number of other words and grammatical constructions, especially the use of the passive voice, reinforce the impression of helplessness that distresses many disabled persons. It is common, for example, to speak of "victims" who "suffer from" or "are afflicted by" various diseases and conditions. The implications of "confined to a wheelchair" for persons who happen to use this mode of transportation are even more objectionable. Collective nouns such as *the handicapped, the blind,* and *the deaf* may be offensive to persons trying to establish their individual worth. They believe that such generalizations are inaccurate, because disabilities vary as much as the persons who have them. Such figures of speech as "wheelchairs" for the people who occupy them emphasizes the aspect of themselves to which these individuals least wish to draw attention.

The general impression of helplessness is reinforced by a widespread tendency to equate disability with illness, although, as one member of a consumer organization observed, "We aren't sick." It is a basic assumption of the medical profession that those whom it serves are "patients." That word implies, first, the endurance of pain or suffering and, secondarily, the recipient of an action or treatment as opposed to the agent who performs it. The role of the patient is a convention that persons who go to the hospital accept as part of the payment for the benefit they expect to receive. Readers who have spent even a short time as patients will remember the demoralizing effect of being deprived of the power to make even the most ordinary decisions, and the relief with which, after their release, they regained control of their own bodily functions, everyday activities, and disposal of time and money. That condition of helplessness may be reinforced by the presuppositions of the social service professions, which find it all too easy to assume that a "client" incapable of earning his living is also incapable of thinking for himself. Many handicapped people, especially those who live in institutions, spend their entire lives in that state of dependence, in spite of efforts to refer to them as "residents," "guests," or "pupils."

Staff members at historical organizations and museums, like people in general, also tend to be confused by many disabilities whose names they know primarily from widely publicized fund-raising campaigns. How many readers, for example, are sure of the difference between muscular dystrophy and multiple sclerosis, or know how either might affect visitors to a museum? Many people also tend to think of these disabilities in terms of their most extreme effects, as an unfor-

tunate side effect of publicity efforts, like the muscular dystrophy telethon, which use severe cases to dramatize the need
for action. On top of that, some people find the sight of physical
deformity disgusting, and most look at handicapped persons
with a certain degree of curiosity. Some disabled persons prefer
to meet that situation head-on by bringing up the subject
themselves. Others are shy, as a result of unfortunate experiences with strangers who regarded them as "freaks."

On the other hand, many people are embarrassed because
they have little experience with disabled persons and are
uncertain how to react in their presence. They are so anxious
not to make mistakes that they may make more than usual,
particularly when performing some unfamiliar task such as
pushing a wheelchair. As a result, museum and historical
society personnel genuinely eager to help handicapped visitors
but uncertain how to do so may hover over them, trying to
anticipate their needs. That approach may make it difficult for
these visitors to do anything for themselves. But most disabled
persons will ask for help when they need it. The staff member or
volunteer need feel no more obligation to press help on them
than on any other visitors.

Many societies today take these matters into consideration within their existing program of museum tours, research
and publication, special events, education and outreach, and
historic preservation. They find that handicapped persons
often participate in these programs as groups from schools,
community centers, and residential facilities, which, like other
organizations, use the resources of historical organizations in
their own programs. Other handicapped visitors appear in
ordinary groups such as public school classes and families,
while a few may come by themselves. All of them are anxious
that their special needs shall not distract anyone—themselves,
the people with them, or society personnel—from the event
that they have come to enjoy. That can best be accomplished by
anticipating obstacles, reducing them as much as possible by
structural or mechanical modifications, and requiring advance
notice for special arrangements. Thus, handicapped persons
will be able to participate in these activities with others in an
integrated setting, which is what they most desire.

4

"Good Ethics, Good Public Relations, Good Business"

MANY museums, while recognizing their legal and moral obligation to serve handicapped persons, wonder if the trouble and expense is justified because they receive few disabled visitors. Many disabled persons are accustomed to take for granted that public places are inaccessible to them because so many have been so in the past. Many come from social and economic levels in which museum visiting is not a normal leisure activity among their relatives and friends. Those who have been disabled from birth have often received scanty education, which has not introduced them to the opportunities for learning and enjoyment offered by museum experiences. In many communities, limitations of transportation, housing, and other services make it very difficult for them to engage in any activities not essential for day-to-day living. In addition, increasing costs and the lack of some services at any price circumscribe their activities in ways that other people find difficult to imagine.

Historical societies are actually in a better position to deal with this situation than major museums, because historical societies are so much a part of their local communities. Their purpose is, after all, preserving, recording, and disseminating the history of the community's unique cultural traditions and experiences, of which handicapped citizens are a part and to which they can contribute as much as anyone else. Through nearby agencies and other organizations, the historical society can invite its handicapped neighbors to become familiar with its resources for discovering the roots of their own experience. In return, it can offer these agencies and organizations a new, conveniently located cultural resource for enriching the lives of the people they serve. As one survey respondent put it, improving access for the disabled is "good ethics, good public relations, good business." It can add a valuable dimension to the historical society's appreciation of the past and contribution to the future of its community.

"Guided According to Their Capacity"

Museums and historic sites that have not had many handicapped visitors often wonder how to conduct tours for such groups. When structural or program modifications have been completed, it is a good idea to invite an appropriate organization to try out the adapted facilities and give staff members and volunteers an opportunity to practice their new skills. Properly publicized in a variety of local media, such a visit will also alert other handicapped people to the museum's accessibility and encourage them to take advantage of it. Activities of this sort, especially when conducted for the first time, require a good deal of advance planning in conjunction with the leaders of the invited group. That planning needs to be thoroughly and carefully done, so that everyone knows what to expect and the visit goes reasonably smoothly. No one thinks everything will go perfectly the first time, but one of the best ways of making disabled persons feel welcome and eager to return is to take their visit as much in stride as those of other groups.

One of the most important elements of this advance planning is a preliminary visit to the historic site by leaders of the handicapped group, including a meeting with the staff members or volunteers who will receive them. These leaders, who should if possible include at least one of the group's disabled members, can survey the premises for obstacles and point out any difficulties they foresee. They can tell the staff something about the limitations of the persons who will be coming and warn them of some individual difficulties. That can be particularly important when some of the visitors have multiple disabilities, such as mentally retarded persons who also have limited vision or mobility. Museum staff members, for their part, can inform the visitors of applicable policies, such as limits on the number of guide dogs or requirements for the supervision of mental patients; and they can brief the group on rules affecting all visitors, such as appropriate behavior; they may also point out rules that may be adjusted to fit circumstances, such as which objects may and may not be touched.

It is also well for staff members and volunteers to have a

meeting among themselves to determine the details of what is to be done. That may include designating the route to be taken by a group in wheelchairs and specifying the number of sub-groups into which the party should be divided. Objects can be selected to be brought downstairs or to be designated for every blind person in a group to touch. The content of interpretation needs to be considered, and some attention given to effective presentation. There can be some thought given to points to be emphasized and participatory experiences to be included for groups with mental limitations. If more than one staff member will be receiving the group, the respective responsibilities of each must be defined and labor divided among them. Various types of emergencies should be foreseen and ways of dealing with them projected, so that all know exactly who, where, and how to call for help if help should be needed.

The impact of such a visit on other activities going on at the same time also needs to be considered. Although handicapped visitors should not be segregated by closing the facility to everyone else while they are present, the unfamiliarity of procedures to both museum personnel and visitors will make everything take more time and create more confusion than anticipated. Normal traffic flow in elevators and hallways may be interrupted, and rest rooms and cafeteria lines may become congested. Disabled persons may become separated from their groups, may have difficulty in finding desired locations, or may behave in a manner disconcerting to other visitors. Children in regular public school groups may distract some handicapped persons by their ordinary noise, or the children may be distracted by their normal curiosity concerning the other visitors. In some parts of the country, winter visits may be further complicated by snow impeding access and the necessity for taking off and putting on outdoor clothing.

Tours by persons in wheelchairs have rather complicated logistics. If the organization visited operates a fairly large open-gallery museum, it may be able to accommodate a bus-load of ten or twelve such visitors. It is important to provide a parking space suitable for operation of the hydraulic lift on the bus and to make sure that there are curb cuts between the parking area and the ramp at the museum entrance. The entire group may be welcomed in a main floor lobby, but should then be subdivided into parties of three or four wheelchairs, each with its own guide. These groups can then set off in different directions; their routes should be carefully mapped in advance to reduce congestion on the elevators. The schedule can be unexpectedly complicated if visitors need to separate from their groups to use rest rooms on another floor. If the bus is to return for them at a specific time, that should be clearly understood by museum personnel when planning the tour, so that everyone can be ready to embark when the bus arrives.

Tours of historic houses should be smaller—not more than four or perhaps six wheelchair visitors, depending on the size of the house and the number of available staff members. To relieve congestion, these groups can be divided into parties of two, each with its own guide. These parties can then circulate from room to room on the first floor before assembling for an audiovisual interpretation of the second story; or, if individuals normally view the first floor on their own, they can go from room to room at their own pace. In a guided tour, it will be necessary for the guides to plan presentations of roughly equal length for each room, so that the groups can move without delay and be ready to assemble at the same time. Maneuvering wheelchairs in cramped, unfamiliar spaces will require the visitors' full attention, so guides should not attempt to continue interpretation while the group are in motion. Guides should, however, be prepared to direct everyone to locations from which all the objects to be described can be seen.

Museum personnel who have conducted tours for the blind stress the importance of adequate pre-visit information and attention to the visitors' individual interests and needs. One historical society has prepared a valuable set of staff guidelines for use on these occasions. A pre-visit questionnaire inquires at what age the visitors have lost their sight and whether they could perceive images, colors, or shapes. It asks whether any have other disabilities—deafness, mental retardation, or limited mobility, including fear of heights. It also inquires whether any of the visitors are not touch-oriented. A preliminary visit by a staff member from the agency for the blind is requested.

Group in wheelchairs enjoys videotape tour of the second story of Trout Hall, Allentown, Pennsylvania.—*Photograph by Andrew Moore*

When groups reach the site, they receive a general orientation, an explanation of the unusual construction of its historic building, and a tour of the collection. The introduction includes an opportunity for the group to become familiar with selected sample artifacts—say, pierced-tin lanterns—by passing several of the objects chosen from hand to hand while the visitors are seated in the orientation room. The visitors then go outside to appreciate the unusual architecture of the structure from the exterior and come back in to get an idea of its interior arrangement. To avoid confusion, the tour focuses on tactile experiences of two or three objects in each room. It lasts about an hour and a half. Finding the initial group of twenty too large, the society plans to divide future tours into parties of not more than eight visitors.

Organizing sign-language tours for deaf groups need not be difficult if the organization visited can locate an interpreter—perhaps a deaf person—interested in learning to be a tour guide. If their availability is publicized through the communication network of local agency newsletters, perhaps in conjunction with Deaf Awareness Week, response is likely to be great, because deaf people have few opportunities for recreation in the community at large. One historical society whose volunteers included an instructor in sign language at a local college initiated such a program, as a bicentennial project. Five of his students volunteered, and historical society personnel trained one or two of them to be tour guides at each of its historic houses. The overwhelming initial response astonished the society's board of directors. Similar tours were thereafter conducted one Saturday a month, but attendance fell off, gradually, because such a large proportion of the deaf people in the area had already enjoyed them.

It is well for guides working with interpreters for the deaf to remember that deaf people think in pictures and have a highly developed capacity for assembling details to form coherent wholes. It is best to tell them, for example, that a room was used for eating or sleeping by certain people at a given time and let them come to their own conclusions about how these things were done with the objects before them, encouraging them to ask questions if they want to know more. The guide can explain the function of particular objects by acting out the functions for which they were used. In a bedroom, for example, one may remove a piece of outer clothing, hang it up, and turn down the bed covering. Then, shivering, one may go to the fireplace, pretend to fill the bed warmer with hot coals, and rub it between the sheets. Then the guide can pretend to blow out a candle, replace the candlestick on the bedside table, and sit down on the bed to answer any questions, in sign language.

Museum visits for retarded persons can be effective if everyone knows exactly what to expect and historic artifacts are presented in the context of familiar everyday activities. One historical society asks the school arranging such a visit to separate retarded pupils beforehand into groups of "educables" and "trainables," to whom guides then adapt their usual presentations for elementary school or preschool children. It recommends that tours be no longer than half an hour and sometimes shorter, and that the presentation be a story showing visitors how they might have used museum objects for familiar activities a long time ago. In the Metropolitan Museum of Art program of repeated visits for retarded adults, a museum staff member first visits the group in its usual meeting place. The group then visits the museum two or three times, always accompanied by the same staff member. Finally, that person visits them again, in their own setting, for a follow-up that includes ingenious techniques by which persons with limited understanding can tell which parts of the visit they enjoyed most.

A historic house in the South held a carefully planned and smoothly executed Christmas party for a group of retarded children. The director sent a large picture of the house to the school before she visited the children in their classroom to get acquainted and give a brief slide presentation. A meeting of teachers, museum staff members, and volunteers allowed those in charge to get acquainted with each other and settle the exact sequence of events. There was a wide variety of activities, including decorating a Christmas tree, listening to a storyteller, and singing favorite songs, which gave the children opportunities to use their physical energy in familiar ways in an unusual setting. A brief tour of the house concentrated on a few large objects, some of which the children were permitted to touch, historical perspective being limited to "before you were born" and "a long time ago." Thus the children enjoyed themselves in a setting in which other people had enjoyed themselves a long time ago, surely a fitting representation of the tradition of hospitality of a Southern plantation.

"We Might Be Able to Develop a Program . . . If We Could Generate Financial Support"

A number of historical societies responded to the survey that few handicapped persons used parts of their facilities already accessible and that that hampered their efforts to raise funds for further improvements. One important reason for such a situation is that many disabled people, who may be more or less isolated from the community and from its normal channels of communication, are not aware of accessible programs. The society should therefore make a point of mentioning accessible features in its brochures and other advertising, perhaps accompanied by a picture showing some person with a visible disability among a group of visitors. The inauguration of adaptations like the tours just described can be publicized in the same way as the opening of an exhibition, with appropriate media coverage. Many consumer groups are delighted to have such publicity for their efforts to improve accessibility in the general community, but others—such as the parents of some handicapped children—regard it as exploitation; the historical organization must of course consult with the visitors in advance and respect their wishes in this matter. Development of an outreach program may include preparation of audiovisual presentations that can be shown at meetings of interested community organizations. Staff members can call successful projects to the attention of other historical societies and museums at meetings and workshops sponsored by regional consortia and the conferences of national organizations such as the American Association for State and Local History.

Redesigning the historical organization's brochure with consideration for the needs of persons with limited vision, hearing, and mental capacity may make it more attractive to a changing general audience. The small print, crowded format, and detailed information of most brochures are discouraging to many casual visitors, especially children. It has been observed in many other contexts that television-oriented generations read far more slowly and command smaller vocabularies and much less general background information than used to be taken for granted. The shift from history to social studies in school curricula means that most young people have little acquaintance with orderly sequences of past events that used to be generally accepted points of reference. There are increasing numbers of Americans, to say nothing of visitors from other countries, to whom standard English is a second language. All of these people will appreciate simply written brochures containing basic information that can be presented on the usual-sized flyer—an 8½-by-11-inch sheet folded in thirds—using large type and ample illustrations. Certain colors of paper and ink may also be confusing to persons with color-blindness and some other visual limitations.

A good brochure should include a single sentence indicating what facilities are available at what times and giving a telephone number to call for further information. The requirement that disabled persons have equal access to the program when viewed in its entirety does not mean that services requiring special equipment or personnel must be available at all times. Since most historic properties require all visitors to tour with a guide and all groups to make advance reservations, these conditions can properly be extended to handicapped individuals and groups. Advance notice can be required for services requiring unusual equipment or personnel, especially when they are infrequently used. They may also be scheduled at intervals, like the monthly tours for the deaf previously described.

It has been observed that some very small historical society museums with few visitors sometimes change their hours without notice. While it is a discourteous inconvenience for anyone to arrive, especially from a distance, at a museum and find it closed, it is a serious imposition on handicapped persons who must often make an unusual effort to get there at all. Even those who live in the community must often arrange in advance for transportation or persons to accompany them. It is therefore a matter of good public relations as well as common courtesy and professional responsibility for museums and historical sites to take seriously the obligation implied by posting stated hours of opening. Changes in these hours should be promptly and accurately reported on bulletin boards, in brochures, printed materials, and publicity releases, and in recordings used on automatic telephone-answering devices. The switchboard operator or any person likely to answer the telephone at the museum or historic site should be fully informed about how to reply to inquiries concerning accommodations for the handicapped or to which staff member such questions should be referred. Information-desk personnel also need complete data and some instruction in recognizing and welcoming persons who may need assistance, particularly those, such as the deaf, whose disability may not be immediately visible and who are sometimes hesitant to call attention to it. It may also be helpful to post a sign in a conspicuous location, announcing that printed materials, cassette recordings, or other forms of assistance are available on request.

Publicity for accessible features need not necessarily be only in the printed word or through pictures and video coverage. One historical society called attention to an underutilized wheelchair that had been donated to it by placing the chair, folded, just inside the front entrance. There, visitors, especially many elderly people, discovered it with astonishment and used it with delight, often asking a friend who accompanied them to push. This argues against the idea that many museum visitors hesitate to use a wheelchair because they fear that persons who see them will jump to the conclusion that they have had some disabling disease. Another, larger museum has purchased for covering its distances three small motorized vehicles, which it often mentions in publicity releases. One society surveyed reported having been donated a walker with a seat, which visitors who need to rest frequently find very helpful.

Media coverage of such events as the first wheelchair tour using a new ramp, elevator, or audiovisual alternative interpretation is often very effective in attracting other handicapped visitors. One museum reported that many disabled visitors came after learning of the availability of its programs from a newspaper article about a wheelchair tour. It is important, however, that facilities and services announced in that way be actually available at the times stated, so that those who come to use them will not be disappointed. It may also be possible to publicize the society's accessibility on a radio or television talk show, especially during national awareness weeks for various disabilities or historic preservation. Such arrangements must be made well in advance with the station or the host of the show. It should be remembered, in planning for television coverage of any event, that the positioning of lights and cameras can be time-consuming and distracting to persons not familiar with video production, although many of them are fascinated with a glimpse behind the scenes.

It is also important to take advantage of existing communications networks among disabled citizens. The use of newsletters for the deaf to promote sign-language tours has already been mentioned. Organizations of disabled consumers, including those with limited mobility, also publish newsletters that would welcome such items. Radio stations operated by or for the blind can be particularly helpful, not merely in announcing events, but in their potential for creative activities in their own right. The interest of some of them in reading and recording local history materials has already been mentioned. Historical society volunteers might also be interested in working with such stations to develop one or more call-in programs featuring older residents' memories of their community's past. Indeed, it has been observed that when local commercial stations have talk-show guests on that subject, the calls received are often of unusually high quality and deserving of the society's attention on general principles.

Historical organizations and museums that develop successful program adaptations should certainly call them to the attention of others in the profession who might like to profit by their experience. The American Association for State and Local History will report such items in the appropriate department of *History News*. The National Information Service for Arts and the Handicapped is actively soliciting information of this nature for its continuing series of publications. *Cornerstone,* the recently founded newsletter of the Small Museums Committee of the American Association of Museums, and the National Trust for Historic Preservation's *Preservation News* would also appreciate news notes of that sort. And regional consortia and state historical associations may also have newsletters that should be informed. In that way, museums and historical organizations can build on each other's accomplishments and mistakes, and miscalculations need not be repeated.

Such programs, especially when conducted in conjunction with agencies serving the handicapped and included in *their* newsletters and publicity, may be very helpful to historical organizations seeking funds for major renovations. Fundraising is, of course, a prime consideration in such projects and is specifically mentioned as one of the steps to be included in the transition plan required by the Section 504 guidelines. Small museums and historical organizations must think very carefully about costs and sources of funds before undertaking new programs of any kind. Some are on such tight budgets that the diversion of even a few tens or hundreds of dollars for improving accessibility requires the sacrifice of something else. Structural alterations cannot be undertaken without funding from outside sources. A directory of public agencies and private foundations interested in proposals to benefit the handicapped is listed in the bibliography of this book.

Small historic organizations as well as large are encouraged to apply for a wide variety of federal grants. The National Endowment for the Arts, in accordance with a specific provision of its charter, has taken a commanding lead in promoting the accessibility of all performing and visual arts, including museums. Museums and historical societies can also apply to the Museums and Historical Organizations Program of the National Endowment for the Humanities. The new HEW Office of Museum Services also has much to offer them. Societies whose collection touches on the history of science, technology, or industry might find it worthwhile to investigate the resources of the National Science Foundation. Survey respondents had received grants, some of them quite substantial, from all of these agencies except the last.

In most states, state as well as federal funds are distributed through a council for the arts, the humanities, or other cultural activities. Education and social service agencies may be interested in co-operative projects of historical organizations and other community agencies. Restoration of historic buildings for use as human resource centers for a variety of community activities, for example, are often financed by such grants. In preparing proposals for such projects, an organization needs to consider its program from all possible angles—historic preservation, education, community service. Museums and historical organizations' places as guardians of the cultural tradition of the entire community make them natural leaders in interpreting that tradition to newcomers, including members of racial and ethnic minorities. One society secured a grant for a very ingenious program to prevent delinquency among rootless minority young people by making them aware of the heritage surrounding them by photographing old buildings. There are many possibilities in such a project for helping young people with various disabilities to participate more fully in the world around them.

As competition grows keener for available funds at all levels of government, museums and historical organizations would be well advised to look to private sources. Local individuals and corporations can often be interested in projects that will benefit both the historical organization and handicapped citizens. Many funding sources find particularly attractive small, single projects with immediately visible results. They often respond to requests for contributions in services or in kind rather than in cash. In seeking such contributions, a local organization takes the lead in working together with others for the benefit of the entire community, as well as of the handicapped. That may not only assist it in raising funds and enhancing its public image, but may also reinforce its position as cornerstone of that community's past and future.

Effective economy in the improvement of accessibility may also include use of shared services available through local and regional consortia. The usefulness of these organizations in holding workshops, providing clearinghouses for the exchange of information, and sponsoring single advisory committees of agencies for the handicapped and individuals for a number of historical organizations have already been mentioned. They can also facilitate sharing of equipment, such as a TTY, or teletypewriter device for telephone communication with the deaf, which could be installed in the consortium office. Deaf persons wishing information about activities of any participating historical organization or museum could then call the consortium office, where a member of the staff there could answer their questions. The consortium could also own a large-type typewriter or other equipment for reproducing materials for the blind; and it might employ a staff member, part-time or full-time, providing technical assistance in improving accessibility.

"This Is Their World, Too"

The recognition that disabled persons have a part to play in local historical organizations is one more step in a fundamental shift in the reason for existence of these groups. Some historical societies were originally limited to descendants of early settlers. Others were founded primarily to preserve a historic structure or a collection of documents or artifacts. Some concentrated on the maintenance of libraries and the publication of antiquarian research. In some communities, historical society membership has been regarded as something of a status symbol, and activities have been primarily social. Staff members and volunteers have therefore expected to devote their principal attention to preserving the collection, promoting research, and carrying out projects of interest to the members.

But in the second half of the twentieth century, historical societies have increasingly recognized their responsibility to serve the entire community whose traditions they preserve. Tax-exempt status and the availability of state and local funds as well as federal government grants have opened new avenues of support, but at the same time created an obligation for the society to give the taxpayers their money's worth in the form of facilities available and services significant to them. The traditional introduction of children to museum resources has been expanded, as curricula of certain grades emphasize state and local history. And ordinary people have learned to use their increased leisure to enjoy their historic heritage, especially as a result of the bicentennial celebration. Because local citizens are proud of the records and relics that preserve and illustrate their community's past, they want to be able to understand these things and explain them to their children. They therefore prefer that historical society staff members and volunteers devote as much attention to displaying, interpreting, and making the collection available to everyone as they do to preserving and increasing it and engaging in activities for members alone.

That change in their reason for being has already prompted some shifts in the emphasis of historical society programs. The development of research libraries and presses at nearby universities has reduced the need for historical societies to sponsor scholarship and publication. Education programs expanded during the population explosion of the 1950s and 1960s are now in less demand, as public school enrollments decline. Museums and historic houses that attracted many tourists at the time of the bicentennial are now facing the limitations of travel created by the rising price of energy. But at the same time, people who have moved frequently are becoming curious about their own roots and the cultural traditions of their new communities, while those who return to the cities and purchase old houses are seeking to preserve the historic heritage of these neighborhoods. So the historical society's audience is now more than ever the entire, fascinatingly diverse population of its locality.

Historical societies may also find their function changing as the American way of life shifts from a period of rising to one of stable or declining expectations. So long as inflation continues, it is to be expected that funds will be increasingly difficult to secure, while the prices of everything the society uses will rise. Like the people who support a historical organization, the organization's administrators will have to make increasingly difficult choices concerning the things they want most to do and those they simply cannot afford. It may be necessary to limit acquisitions, revise restoration plans, reduce staff, and curtail services. In these circumstances, it is fortunate that most modifications for the benefit of disabled persons also increase the efficiency of operations and improve services to everyone. By increasing a historical organization's usefulness as a cultural resource in its community, these modifications, as it has already been pointed out, may assist the organization in raising the funds it needs for these other purposes.

It is also clear that the continuing energy crisis will make great changes in community living patterns. People will move back into the cities and share housing, in order to reduce transportation and heating costs. They will travel less and will be looking for leisure activities within walking distance or in easy reach by mass transit. Museums and historical organizations can expect fewer visitors from a distance and more from their own neighborhoods. Public schools will arrange fewer field trips, but may be even more interested in outreach programs, especially those encouraging children to participate in the process of historic preservation. The improvement of mass transit for disabled persons may bring more of them to museums, particularly those whose interest has been aroused by outreach programs.

But economic stringency may represent a challenge to museums and historical organizations, as well as a curtailment of programs. Reduction of employment and limitation of income may inspire people to devise less expensive ways of accomplishing the things they want to do. Older people who remember the Great Depression of the 1930s recall many examples of inventive ingenuity that no one would have dreamed possible until they were necessary—when they were accomplished. Local historical organizations might well make a practical contribution to present-day problems by collecting the memories of older people for the benefit of younger ones who have never had to think in these terms. At the same time, such organizations may benefit disabled persons who all too often have lived on severely limited resources for some time.

As limited resources compel many organizations to rely more than ever on volunteer help, many will want to explore the contribution that disabled members can make in that capacity. Some disabled persons may wish to help in the office or library, while others handy with tools may be able to learn simple conservation skills, as in several workshops for mentally retarded persons that produce reproductions of regional or period furniture for the market. Some volunteer workers with disabilities will not wish to face the general public, but others may enjoy doing so, in the gift shop or at the information desk, as exhibit guards or tour guides. Here, however, the institution will have to consider not merely the interests of the volunteers and the implementation of its own policies, but the attitudes of other visitors and the community in general. It will be necessary for the organization's staff members and the handicapped volunteers to think through together fully and frankly the probable consequences of all possible courses of action. Curtailments of staff may make it more difficult than ever to hire disabled employees but, as has already been pointed out, historical organizations that have employed disabled persons have found them invaluable.

Museums and historical organizations today often find themselves at a crossroads between past and future, wondering what direction they should take. Half of those surveyed have been founded within the last quarter-century, many in anticipation of or under the impetus of the bicentennial. Although that celebration is now history, its effects, like those of the centennial of 1876, are only beginning to be felt. That event focused upon the Philadelphia Exposition and, emphasizing the origins of national unity in the wake of the divisions of the Civil War, steered the historical understanding of Americans into a path of liberty, equality, and homogeneity that shaped their view of their country and that which they communicated to children, immigrants, and foreigners for generations afterward. The bicentennial, by contrast, focused upon a wide variety of local activities held together by a few nationally televised events, stressed diversity, respect for the views of others, and unity achieved when important by individual choice, reflecting aspects of the character of Americans that will certainly shape the future. As one of the most important results of the centennial was the rediscovery of much of the American past, so the bicentennial can demonstrate how that past can be used as a foundation and a source of tools and materials for building the future. Now, local historical organizations and museums can help to demonstrate how that process takes place in every community as well as in the nation as a whole.

Although the bicentennial gave great impetus to historic preservation, that movement has been well under way for two generations. Federal public assistance projects during the Great Depression preserved many regional crafts and collected a great deal of local folklore, while one of the great American fortunes reconstructed Colonial Williamsburg as a model of painstaking historic restoration. After World War II, which brought citizen soldiers into contact with monuments preserved all over the world, similar efforts were made to maintain and restore historic buildings in this country. At first, as abroad, these were likely to be the mansions of the wealthy or the homes of famous persons, appreciated by visitors who viewed with awe and admiration their trend-setting architecture, costly collections of works of fine art, or beautiful examples of the finest styles of decoration. The way of life of ordinary

people has been preserved, as in Europe, as museums of folk art
or depictions of the hardships endured by early pioneers from
which their descendants escaped by hard work and persever-
ance. At present, historic preservation includes the full range
of activities by which people of all origins and backgrounds
earned their living, traveled from place to place, and engaged
in everyday domestic and leisure activities.

One result of the bicentennial and of this movement for
historic preservation is the discovery among Americans of all
backgrounds of the roots in their historic heritage—of their
personal as well as their national identity. Many historical
society members are participating in the grass-roots interest in
genealogy that has transformed that study from the pursuit of
illustrious ancestors to the tracing of sequences of ordinary
lives. Once lines of descent have been established, many inves-
tigators turn to filling out the biographies of individuals so
identified and reconstructing the context of their daily lives.
For that work, they are learning to use not merely written
records in libraries, but artifacts of material culture in
museum collections and in preserved, restored, or reconstructed historic houses and other environments. Many individuals turn from the study of museum collections to the
preservation of the homes, districts, and furnishings with
which they live. Young people settling in the cities for reasons
of economy are reviving whole neighborhoods previously con-
demned to destruction and setting a worthwhile example for
others who live there. Since so many poor people live in old
houses, the part of historical organizations in this movement
can place them in the forefront of a many-sided impetus for
civic improvement.

By assisting in this rediscovery of personal and local roots,
the historical organization can also participate in the reinforcement of important national values. For generations,
American children were initiated into the traditions of liberty,
equality, and homogeneity in required American history
courses. Now, in many schools, these courses have been replaced by more generalized social studies, which leave many
pupils with little sequential understanding of their nation's
past. These young people are becoming aware that they have

missed something, and they want to find out how traditional values have shaped the world in which they live. Activities of historical organizations can help them see how the general principles that they learn in school have been applied in familiar situations and locations. Thus historical organizations can create in the next generation the interest that will support such programs in years to come.

All these concerns of the general community are also concerns of its handicapped members, who have lived with some of them every day for many years. Handicapped members may therefore contribute even more to local historical organizations than they will gain from the organization's accessible programs. An important function of any repository of relics and records is to discover new ways in which its collection can be used and enjoyed, and disabled people bring a variety of unusual insights to that creative process. Another function is to go beyond documents and material culture to maintain the living tradition that has made a community what it is and will shape its response to future events, in which handicapped citizens will play an ever-increasing part. More and more, a present-minded generation is discovering that there can be no foresight without memory, no future without a past, as a tree must have roots and a building a firm foundation. As the nation enters upon the uncertainties of its third century, disabled individuals join with the rest of their diverse countrymen to preserve the historic heritage of their communities as a major source of strength of the American people.

Appendixes
Bibliography
Index

Appendix A–The Law

The following are excerpts from the Rehabilitation Act of 1973 and the implementation guidelines for Section 504 of that law.

Section 504 of the Rehabilitation Act of 1973 (Public Law 93-112, 29 U.S.C. 794), Section 504, provides that "no otherwise qualified handicapped individual shall, solely by reason of his handicap, be excluded from the participation in, be denied the benefits of or be subjected to discrimination under any program or activity receiving federal financial assistance."

National Endowment for the Arts Implementation Guidelines for Section 504 S 1151.22 Existing Facilities:

(A) A recipient shall operate each program or activity to which this part applies so that the program or activity, *when viewed in its entirety,* is readily accessible to and usable by handicapped persons. This paragraph *does not require a recipient to make each of its existing facilities or every part of a facility accessible* to and usable by handicapped persons. (Emphasis added.)

(B) ... A recipient is not required to make structural changes in existing facilities where other methods are effective in achieving compliance ...

(C) *Time period.* A recipient shall comply with the requirements of Paragraph A of this section within sixty days of the effective date of this part, except that when structural changes are necessary to make programs or activities in existing facilities accessible, such changes shall be made as soon as possible but not in any event later than three years after the effective date of this part.

(D) *Transition plan.* In the event structural changes to facilities are necessary to meet the requirements of Paragraph A ... The plan shall be developed with the assistance of interested persons, including handicapped persons or organizations representing handicapped persons.

Department of Interior Guidelines for Programs Involving Historic Properties 17.64:

... In providing accessibility in historic properties, the fullest accessibility will be provided to the handicapped as is possible consistent with the principles of programs involving historic properties, to preserve historical features of these facilities. When it is not reasonable to make building alterations or structural changes to historic properties, other methods of providing accessibility may include, but are not limited to:

(1) Construction of new facilities . . .

(2) Reassigning programs to accessible locations.

(3) Delivering programs or activities at alternative accessible sites operated by or available for such use by the recipient.

(4) Assignment of aides to Beneficiaries.

(5) Other methods that result in making the program or activity accessible to handicapped persons.

(b) To the maximum extent possible, alterations and structural changes necessary to achieve accessibility shall be undertaken so as not to alter or destroy architecturally significant elements or features of the properties.

"Historic Properties" shall mean those properties listed in or eligible for listing in the National Register of Historic Places or properties designated under a statute of the appropriate state or local governmental body.

Statement of National Advisory Council on Historic Preservation, *Federal Register,* February 13, 1980:

In the case of historic properties, program accessibility shall mean that, when viewed in their entirety, programs are accessible to and usable by handicapped persons. After all other methods of providing access have been examined and found unsatisfactory in achieving access, recipients of federal assistance may find it necessary to make alterations to historic properties. Certain alterations may cause a significant impairment of historic features. Historic properties are those which are listed or eligible for listing in the National Register of Historic Places.

Substantial impairment occurs when a permanent alteration is made which results in the significant loss of integrity of finish, materials, design quality, or spatial character. Where access cannot be achieved without causing a significant impairment of historic features, the recipient may seek a modification of waiver of access standards of responsible federal agencies. A decision to seek a modification or waiver should be based on consideration of the following factors:

A. Scale of the structure, reflecting its ability to absorb alterations.

B. Use of the structure, whether primarily for public or private purposes.

C. Importance of the historic features of the structure to the conduct of the program.

D. Cost of alterations as compared to the increase in accessibility.

The decision by the responsible federal agency to grant a modification or waiver of access standards is subject to Section 106 of the National Historic Preservation Act and shall be made in accordance with 36 CFR, part 800. Where the structure is federally owned or where federal funds may be used for alterations, the comments of the council shall be obtained, pursuant to 36 CFR, part 800, prior to the approval of such work by the responsible federal agency.

Appendix B

Responses to Survey of Historical Society Accessibility

Responses by region	New England	Mid States	South	Midwest	Far West	Total
	43	69	46	77	51	286
	(38%)	(48%)	(31%)	(36%)	(51%)	(38%)

Responses by size of society	Member-ship unknown	−200 members	200–500 members	500–1000 members	1000+ members	Total
	16	51	104	68	47	286
	(5%)	(13%)	(33%)	(23%)	(16%)	(100%)

PERCENTAGES BY SIZE OF SOCIETY

	Member-ship unknown	−200 members	200–500 members	500–1000 members	1000+ members	Total
Date of founding						
Before 1850	12	2			6	2
1851-1900		2	14	24	38	17
1901-1925		4	12	25	14	13
1926-1950		6	21	17	12	14
Since 1951	54	86	57	33	26	48
Area served						
Town or city	12	44	42	30	10	30
County	12	38	58	64	30	46
Several counties	6	8	8	8	10	8
State	18	12	3	17	42	16
Programs						
Library	30	48	69	85	70	63
Museum	42	76	88	93	72	78
Guided tours	36	64	87	83	44	68
Publications	24	62	76	83	74	68
Outreach	36	22	29	42	62	35
Historic preservation	36	76	72	75	54	65
Special events	42	68	72	72	72	64

[Continued on pages 108–109]

Educational program	48	60	81	81	72	70
Site marking	18	34	35	33	34	31
Other	18	14	14	5	14	11
Types of facilities						
Headquarters	30	16	23	42	44	29
Separate library		4	9	9	8	6
Separate museum	6	30	34	21	28	26
Historic houses	36	36	42	54	42	41
Museum village	18	2	3	6	8	5
Other historic structures	18	26	23	14	20	19
Other	12	18	16	15	28	17
Historic district	24	18	31	39	30	29
Architectural accessibility						
Approach and enter	36	54	73	74	64	63
Reach all floors	24	30	18	37	50	29
Alternative interpretation	18	24	17	25	22	20
Accommodations for visual and hearing impairments						
Braille labels			4	3	2	2
Braille brochures		6	3		6	3
Large-type labels		8	18	18	10	13
Large-type brochures			2		6	2
Recorded labels	6		3		6	2
Recorded brochures			11	1.5		4
Readers in library		2	18	14	2	10
Recorded publications			2		2	1
Electronic amplification		2				.3
Staff trained/lip-reading		8	3			2
Printed descriptions		12	24	16	8	15
Sign language	6		2	5	2	2
Activities for mentally limited						
Retarded		8	13	23	10	12
Mentally ill		4	6	12	6	6
Learning disabled	6	8	12	19	6	11
Other	6	4	1		2	1
Staff						
Professional: full-time	36	30	57	68	68	62
Professional: part-time	24	22	26	50	30	30
Professional: disabled		2	6	8	10	6
Nonprofessional: full-time	30	24	28	49	50	31
Nonprofessional: part-time	36	32	40	49	38	38
Nonprofessional: disabled	6		3	3	6	3
Volunteers: Guides	12	30	57	69	48	48
Volunteers: Other	6	22	39	51	36	36
Volunteers: Disabled	12	4	11	11	6	8
Federal funds:						
Architectural renovation	18	12	9	12	18	12

Program activities	24	4	4	5	14	7
NEA	12		6	8	8	6
NEH	24	6	10	16	18	12
HEW Office of Museum Services		1	3	10	3	
ASF						---
CETA	18	24	47	51	42	39
Revenue-sharing	12	18	28	36	18	24
Other		8	13	12	14	11
Section 504 compliance						
Appoint compliance officer	18	12	12	15	18	13
Advisory committee		4	7	12	4	6
Self-evaluation		20	29	30	32	25
Program adaptations		6	9	9	16	9
Transition plan	18		13	18	16	12
Employment procedure review	12	4	10	9	12	9
Board participation	12	20	21	14	14	16
Co-operation with organizations serving the handicapped						
Social service agencies	6	6	13	14	18	12
Rehabilitation centers	6	2	10	12	10	8
Senior citizen centers	18	18	48	48	30	36
Residential facilities	12	4	7	6		5
Consumer organizations	12	6	10	15	12	10
Other		8	13	6	2	7
Publicity mentions accessibility						
Brochures	6	6	5	6	14	7
Advertising		6	1	3	2	2
Releases/special events		14	7	8	8	8
Affiliation						
State historical society	36	46	58	35	28	41
Regional consortia	18	30	45	49	12	34
Co-operative services	6	8	7	12	2	7
Obstacles to handicapped access						
Inaccessible facilities	12	28	41	12	36	28
Insufficient funds	18	44	69	62	30	50
Insufficient information		16	26	18	8	17
Insufficient staff	18	30	60	53	36	43
Handicapped not interested	6	34	38	38	14	30
Nondisabled not interested	6	8	20	17	14	14
Other	6	6	4		6	4
Programs for handicapped						
Limited mobility		8	3	6	4	4
Limited hearing		2			4	1
Limited vision		2		2	4	1
Mental limitations		2	1	5		2
Elderly		20	13	8	8	11

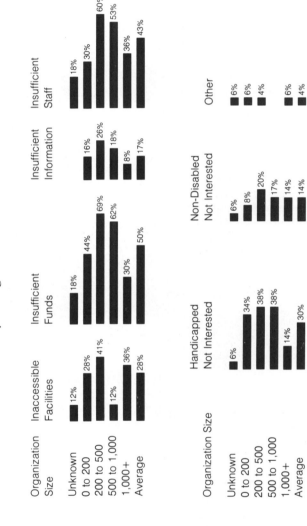

Accessibility Survey:
Percentages of Organizations Surveyed
Reporting Obstacles to Access

Organization Size | Inaccessible Facilities | Insufficient Funds | Insufficient Information | Insufficient Staff

Unknown — 12% | 18% | 16% | 18%
0 to 200 — 28% | 44% | 26% | 30%
200 to 500 — 41% | 69% | 18% | 60%
500 to 1,000 — 12% | 62% | 8% | 53%
1,000+ — 36% | 30% | 17% | 36%
Average — 28% | 50% | | 43%

Organization Size | Handicapped Not Interested | Non-Disabled Not Interested | Other

Unknown — 6% | 6% | 6%
0 to 200 — 34% | 8% | 6%
200 to 500 — 38% | 20% | 4%
500 to 1,000 — 38% | 17% |
1,000+ — 14% | 14% | 6%
Average — 30% | 14% | 4%

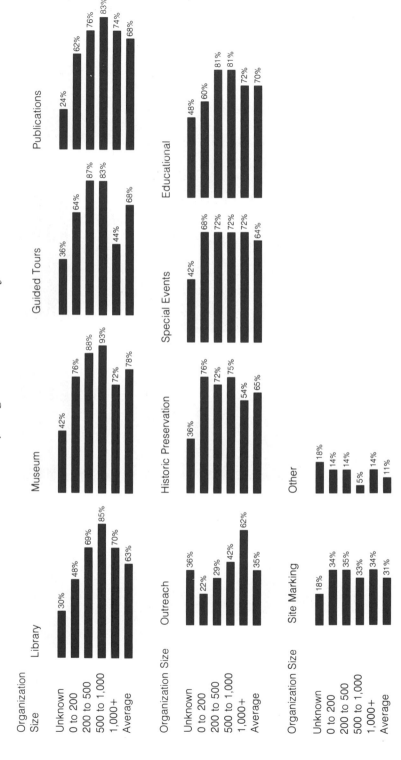

Accessibility Survey:
Programs Offered by Percentages
Of Organizations Surveyed

Organization
Size   Library

Unknown   30%
0 to 200   48%
200 to 500   69%
500 to 1,000 85%
1,000+   70%
Average   63%

Museum

Unknown   42%
0 to 200   76%
200 to 500   88%
500 to 1,000 93%
1,000+   72%
Average   78%

Guided Tours

Unknown   36%
0 to 200   64%
200 to 500   87%
500 to 1,000 83%
1,000+   44%
Average   68%

Publications

Unknown   24%
0 to 200   62%
200 to 500   76%
500 to 1,000 83%
1,000+   74%
Average   68%

Organization Size   Outreach

Unknown   36%
0 to 200   22%
200 to 500   29%
500 to 1,000 42%
1,000+   62%
Average   35%

Historic Preservation

Unknown   36%
0 to 200   76%
200 to 500   72%
500 to 1,000 75%
1,000+   54%
Average   65%

Special Events

Unknown   42%
0 to 200   68%
200 to 500   72%
500 to 1,000 72%
1,000+   72%
Average   64%

Educational

Unknown   48%
0 to 200   60%
200 to 500   81%
500 to 1,000 81%
1,000+   72%
Average   70%

Organization Size   Site Marking

Unknown   18%
0 to 200   34%
200 to 500   35%
500 to 1,000 33%
1,000+   34%
Average   31%

Other

Unknown   18%
0 to 200   14%
200 to 500   14%
500 to 1,000 5%
1,000+   14%
Average   11%

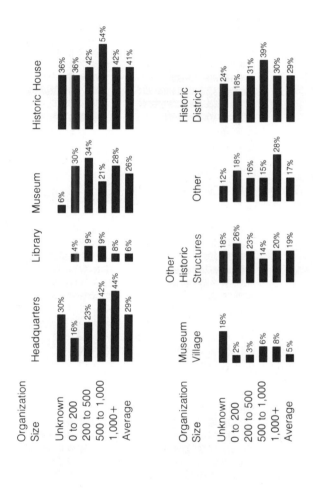

Accessibility Survey:
Types of Facilities Maintained
By Percentages of Organizations Surveyed

Organization
Size

Unknown
0 to 200
200 to 500
500 to 1,000
1,000+
Average

Headquarters
30%
16%
23%
42%
44%
29%

Library
4%
9%
9%
8%
6%

Museum
6%
30%
34%
21%
28%
26%

Historic House
36%
36%
42%
54%
42%
41%

Organization
Size

Unknown
0 to 200
200 to 500
500 to 1,000
1,000+
Average

Museum
Village
18%
2%
3%
6%
8%
5%

Other
Historic
Structures
18%
26%
23%
14%
20%
19%

Other
12%
18%
16%
15%
28%
17%

Historic
District
24%
18%
31%
39%
30%
29%

Accessibility Survey:
Types of Staff Personnel Employed
By Percentage of Organizations Surveyed

Professional Staff

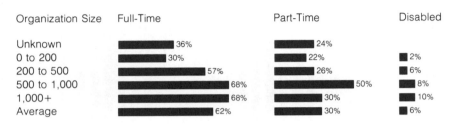

Organization Size	Full-Time	Part-Time	Disabled
Unknown	36%	24%	
0 to 200	30%	22%	2%
200 to 500	57%	26%	6%
500 to 1,000	68%	50%	8%
1,000+	68%	30%	10%
Average	62%	30%	6%

Non-Professional Staff

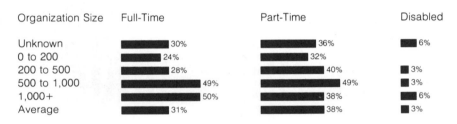

Organization Size	Full-Time	Part-Time	Disabled
Unknown	30%	36%	6%
0 to 200	24%	32%	
200 to 500	28%	40%	3%
500 to 1,000	49%	49%	3%
1,000+	50%	38%	6%
Average	31%	38%	3%

Volunteer Staff

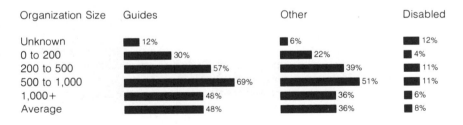

Organization Size	Guides	Other	Disabled
Unknown	12%	6%	12%
0 to 200	30%	22%	4%
200 to 500	57%	39%	11%
500 to 1,000	69%	51%	11%
1,000+	48%	36%	6%
Average	48%	36%	8%

Appendix C

Representative Programs at Historical Organizations

I. Integrated Activities

Founded in 1907, the twenty-member Paul Revere Memorial Association of Boston, Massachusetts, preserves and exhibits the Paul Revere House. After merging with the Moses Pierce Association in 1970, the Revere Association assumed responsibility for the adjoining Moses Pierce-Hichborn House (1711–1716). A director, four professionals, and three to five seasonal interpreters operate interpretative programs for the general public. Entry fees support the maintenance and operation of the house and an extensive off-season educational program for school groups visiting Boston and for Boston neighborhood children. The Paul Revere House is a co-operating member of the Boston National Historic Park.

Like other period buildings, the Paul Revere House encounters a variety of limitations in providing interpretation for disabled visitors. The interpretative program is flexible, designed to meet the varying interests of visitors in general. That has made it possible for the staff to respond quickly and easily to the needs of disabled persons.

The chief problem is access for persons using wheelchairs or other aids to mobility. General admission is through a gate area away from the house. Wheelchair visitors arriving there are invited to enter by the front door, which has only a low sill and is usually used as an emergency exit. The interpreter on the first floor, who is expected at all times to be aware of outside activity, is thus able to admit visitors through this door and to assist them if necessary. Inside, the first floor is accessible to wheelchairs, although a problem may arise on busy days, when a person entering by the front door is obliged to move against the general flow of visitor traffic. There is space outside the traffic area for visitors to rest in the exhibit rooms.

Steep and narrow stairs make the second floor inaccessible to persons in wheelchairs, although some visitors using crutches and canes do go there. Access to that part of the house is currently under study, and improvements are expected in the next three to five years. At present, a photo portfolio and written information is available to visitors who cannot climb the stairs. Since interpretation includes much extemporaneous discussion between the staff and all visitors, the conversations that usually take place with disabled persons are not "special" treatment.

The narrative time-line trail, a back-lighted film strip captioned in bold-face type, has proven very valuable in interpretation for visitors with limited hearing or vision. Written materials are available for deaf visitors when detailed questions arise. A number of printed materials are also available routinely for all visitors, including the deaf. Staff members are asked to offer but not force upon blind visitors the opportunity to enter the exhibit area proper and touch the building and items from the collection. Local agencies have encouraged that method of interpretation, rather than Braille materials, and it has proven very successful.

All groups, including groups of disabled visitors, are encouraged to make advance reservations. Particular attention is paid to establishing communication with the escorts of such groups. In that way, we learn, for example, whether sign-language interpreters will be needed or whether a group of retarded visitors requires an abbreviated tour. To date, the experience with all handicapped groups has been excellent.

Regular training is offered the permanent staff—and the seasonal staff, when possible—through the Boston National Historical Park. The most effective method has brought members of the park's Special Populations Office to the site to consider its special problems with the staff. Many of the personnel at that office are themselves disabled, as well as being professional interpreters. In general, we encourage our staff to work with handicapped visitors as they would with any visitors having a particular area of concern. Our approach is shaped in large part by our desire to communicate our own deep interest in our subject. We do not pretend to be immune from the "handicap" of diffidence and discomfort many people feel with disabled persons. However, the fact that a number of the staff have some disabilities helps us to overcome many of the usual problems. Our objective is to communicate our interest and to aid visitors who need help without smothering or embarrassing them.

II. Access to Varied Historic Structures

The century-old Nebraska State Historical Society is charged with the responsibility of preserving and recording the history of Nebraska and making it available to everyone. The society's headquarters and its newly acquired museum in Lincoln will be made accessible for disabled persons. Of its twenty-three properties throughout the state—all of them on the National Register of Historic Places—six can accommodate disabled visitors. These include the veterinary hospital; the blacksmith, harness repair, and wheelwright's shops at Fort Robinson; the Burlington depot at Red Cloud; and, at Brownville, the dredge *Captain Meriwether Lewis* (main deck only).

The Nebraska State Historical Society has just started removing barriers to the handicapped in some of its buildings. At Fort Robinson, the

1905–1906 blacksmith and harness repair shops, two identical buildings fifty feet apart, were made accessible by constructing entrance ramps. Platforms 5 feet by 6 feet in front of each door were connected by a 4-foot-wide sidewalk. A long, sloping two-stage ramp leads to a proposed parking lot 148 feet away and 4½ feet lower than the floors of the shops. The slope is nowhere steeper than 1 inch in 1 foot, nor is any ramp longer than 30 feet.

After operating a seasonal mobile museum for ten years in a trailer at a highway rest stop near Chimney Rock, the society had a new, accessible trailer constructed for the Chimney Rock site. The new trailer was brought 6 inches closer to ground level by setting the wheels in wheel wells rather than under the floor. A mound of earth was raised in front of the trailer and a ramp and sidewalk paved into it. Brackets attached to the side of the trailer hold a ramp 40 inches wide and 6 feet long, whose last 18 inches are a hinged plate. Experience has shown that placing the staffing angle irons on the top side of the ramp would have provided an additional safety feature for wheelchair users. Built of ⅛-inch steel, designed for a load of 100 pounds per square foot, and equipped with 45-inch-high removable side rails, the ramp is too heavy to be moved by a single person.

A solid security door 36 inches wide, which swings outward, is open while the museum is open, unless there is a severe storm. For additional security, there is a long deadbolt lock on the door, plus the lock on the knob. At each entrance is an inward-swinging screen door, with its lower half covered by plexiglas to prevent the escape of air-conditioned air. These doors are closed by a hinge with a coiled spring around the hinge pin to eliminate the need for a spring in the middle of the door. An unintended half-inch threshold arising from a misunderstanding in construction emphasizes the need for giving builders of unusual adaptations extremely exact specifications.

In 1976 the society received a former Army Corps of Engineers vessel, the *Captain Meriwether Lewis*. This 270-by-85-foot sidewheel steamer was one of two dustpan dredges built in 1932 to open the Missouri River to navigation. It was determined that the boat would be drydocked and cradled with ramps in order to make it accessible to persons in wheelchairs. An elevator or lift is planned to bypass steep steps from the main deck to the boiler deck of the boat, where the main exhibits will be located. That will not provide access to the pilot house or the hurricane deck, but it will permit visitors with limited mobility to reach the most important areas.

All outside doors in the boat have 6-inch-high thresholds, which it would be prohibitively expensive to remove entirely. At two of the five 8-foot-wide sliding doors on the main deck, a 40-inch-wide section has been cut from the steel threshold. Combined with a widening of interior doorways, that will permit total access to the main deck of the dredge. These notches in the thresholds will also make it easier for the maintenance staff to move equipment on and off the boat. The approach to be taken to the 26 public-use doors and 5 crew doors on the boiler deck has not yet been determined. The historical society is forming an advisory committee of disabled persons for consultation on this problem and adequate access to its other buildings, after which it will seek funds to carry out the plans so made.

III. An Accessible Museum Village

The Macon County Museum Complex in Decatur, Illinois, is sponsored by the 850-member Macon County Historical Society, founded in 1916. In 1973 the first museum was opened in an abandoned 1916 church, which is now the folk art center. The new exhibit center consists of six exhibit galleries, plus administrative offices and work spaces in a converted elementary school. The museum has an extensive educational and outreach program—school tours, educators' workshops, and traveling museum kits.

The Macon County Museum Complex is committed to making all of its facilities available to disabled visitors. The exhibit center, opened in 1979, was designed to meet the criteria with interior and exterior ramps, accessible rest rooms, and Braille and raised-letter signs in appropriate locations. The ramps were funded by an HUD community-block grant. Plans are underway to make the former museum, now a folk art center, accessible as soon as funds can be secured.

Perhaps the most novel area of accessibility is the three-acre Prairie Village. The village, consisting of actual historic buildings and reproductions that are being brought to the site, depicts the 1860–1890 era. All roads and walkways will be usable by persons with limited mobility. As buildings are prepared for exhibit, they are made as accessible as possible without damaging extant historical and architectural elements. Ramps are constructed as needed, and if existing doors are too narrow for wheelchairs, stoops or porches are built to permit seated persons to look in doors and windows to see the interior and participate in interpretation. In addition, raised-letter and Braille signs will be installed for the visually impaired. Ramp and porch construction was designed as an integral part of each building's plan, in such a manner as to be harmonious with other buildings in the village and so as not to distract from enjoyment of the village by the undisabled visitor.

Accomplishment of this goal does add to the cost of the development, but it will provide total compliance with Section 504. As this is the only museum in the area depicting the history of the region at that period, the staff consider it mandatory that they serve the entire population, including the disabled.

IV. Producing Videotape Alternative Interpretation

Founded in 1904, the Lehigh County Historical Society in Allentown, Pennsylvania, has more than a thousand members. Besides its office and library in the old Lehigh County courthouse, it maintains four historic houses in and near the city. As part of its participation in Museum Access from 1977 to 1979, the society made two of these houses wheelchair-accessible by installing ramps. It also prepared a videotape interpretation of the second story of Trout Hall, the eighteenth-century mansion of James

Allen, the founder of Allentown. For 1980, it has budgeted funds to improve accessibility at the home of George Taylor, a signer of the Declaration of Independence, through the installation of new sloping walkways from the parking lot and a ramp at the rear entrance.

The Lehigh County Historical Society's videotape interpretation of the second story of Trout Hall was produced and directed by its executive director, who had experience in professional television. It was filmed by a volunteer who owned the necessary camera and editing equipment. The performers were two members of the society's guild of volunteer guides. The chairman of the history department at a local college provided historical continuity.

The filming was preceded by a single two-hour meeting of these five people to explain procedure and agree upon content. No formal script was prepared, partly because amateur performers are likely to sound as if such scripts are "memorized" and partly because such a presentation would be out of keeping with that of the guides showing the first floor. Instead, the guides were asked to adapt those parts of their usual interpretation that they considered most appropriate. They were asked to think beyond information about people and artifacts to ways in which they could vary the visual image by moving from place to place, demonstrating the use of objects, and conversing with each other. They were advised to walk through this presentation together at the museum two or three times before the filming, to prevent hesitation and suggest additional actions.

The structure of the film was determined by the limits of its fifteen-minute time span. Since two minutes were required for an introduction and three for a conclusion, about two-and-a-half minutes could be allowed for each of the four rooms to be depicted. That meant about 250 words for each, describing five principal visual images. These included a general view of each room, a demonstration of an activity that would have taken place there, and close-ups of one or two significant objects.

After this preparation, the actual filming was completed smoothly in a single afternoon. Since the one camera had to be moved from room to room, several takes were necessary. There was some difficulty with adequate lighting, which might be less with improved equipment now on the market. The performers responded well to simple directions about facing the camera and projecting their voices toward the audio equipment. The inevitable mistakes were removed in the editing process, but, as often happens with amateurs, the first take was usually the best.

In the completed videotape, a costumed guide welcomed the visitors at the door and conducted them up the stairs, pausing to comment on some objects displayed on the landing. At the top, the other guide met her to show the way to two bedrooms, the children's room, and a nineteenth-century sitting room. Demonstrations included a chat over tea, a game of cards, and the use of a sewing bird. A music box in the children's room provided authentic musical accompaniment.

Although portable videotape equipment is rapidly becoming easily available, most museum staff members are not skilled in its use. They may find it more practical to locate an individual, corporation, or television station willing to contribute the necessary equipment and expertise. A grant may be secured to cover the cost of these services, or they may be donated as a worthwhile community project. It is necessary to plan carefully so that the resources of highly trained technicians available for a brief period can be used to the greatest advantage. The expense of this videotape was minimal, because equipment was lent and all concerned donated their services, so the only actual cost was for videotape cassettes. The major item of projection equipment was paid for by a grant from a local foundation.

Those who have seen this videotape have enjoyed it very much, and it has an immediacy impossible with pictures or slides. Slides, however, appear to be preferable for close-ups of individual objects and significant details. The expense of projection equipment is justified if it can also be used for other activities. It would be worthwhile for organizations interested in experimenting with the use of videotape in their general programs to consider this form of alternative interpretation. Others can get satisfactory results with slides interpreted by the guide or by a cassette tape.

V. Considering Visitors with Limited Vision

Founded in 1963, the Fulton County Historical Society of Rochester, Indiana, maintains four museums. That in the civic center, which also houses the society's offices, is open year-round; the others operate only in the summer. The society sponsors local folk culture festivals and emphasizes folk materials in its publications. These include a quarterly and occasional original volumes, as well as reprints of local histories and genealogies. Special attention has been given to the history and genealogy of the Potawatomi Indians, who lived in the area until their removal in 1838 and were among the ancestors of many local residents.

We use the following rules to help persons with limited vision appreciate our exhibits.

1. Hang pictures with writing or small details lower than big pictures with big details. Hang small pictures at the eye level of people five feet tall. That way, children can look up, and tall people can look down, and the majority can see it.

2. Do not use fancy lettering, as it is distinctly hard to read. Make signs with "primary print," the kind of printing a first-grade teacher uses on the blackboard. Avoid script and modern, puffy-type styles.

3. Be sure light is adequate. People with cataracts need more light, and even near-sighted people find it hard to read in half light. Make sure the light does not glare off the glass, making it impossible to see through the glass.

4. Place dark objects on light backgrounds, such as white paper or paint. That makes them easier to see, even if the light is not perfect.

5. Don't place words less than one inch tall above a height of five feet, because people wearing bifocals have to look down, not up, to read.

VI. Craft Participation for Handicapped Children

Rocky Mount Historical Association in Tennessee was founded in 1959 to preserve, restore, and furnish the nine-room log house that served as the capitol of the Southwest Territory from 1790 to 1792. The association now has more than 450 members. The historic site occupies fifteen acres in the hills of upper East Tennessee. It includes the Cobb-Massengill House, built between 1770 and 1772, a detached kitchen, smokehouse, slave cabins, and a barn. A modern regional museum was built nearby to help interpret the site. Visitors are shown through the site by trained, costumed guides. Large groups are encouraged to make reservations.

Including disabled visitors in the educational program has been an easy task for Rocky Mount, partly because of the experience the staff have had in handling groups of all ages and abilities. Since it opened, Rocky Mount has told thousands of people the story of Tennessee's founding and has tried various ways of interpreting pioneer life. In 1975, Rocky Mount began "Craft Days," a hands-on experience of pioneer living that teaches fireplace cooking, spinning, wool processing, candle-making, pewter casting, log-hewing, and more. Each year the list of activities changes.

Built-in flexibility is another element in Rocky Mount's success with handicapped groups. Although only three to six crafts are taught at a time, Rocky Mount offers a choice of eleven crafts, ranging in difficulty from dipping candles to casting pewter. This range allows the program to be tailored to the students' abilities. For example, a class of blind students might spin flax, make candles, and process wool. A class of retarded children might cook on the fireplace, harvest the eighteenth-century garden, and dye wool with vegetable dyes. Deaf students might do any of the crafts, provided a teacher-interpreter was assigned to each group.

Finally, planning is the key. When reservations are made, the teacher consults with Rocky Mount's education director, to decide which crafts would be best for the group. Then preparations are made. The teacher tells the students what to expect and what will be expected of them. The education director selects craft instructors and informs them of the students' special requirements, along with any instructions from the teacher. Safety is a big consideration during the planning. For that reason, the groups are limited to six students per instructor, and crafts are selected that the students can complete safely and successfully within a reasonable length of time. If necessary, however, additional time is allowed. Simply by letting handicapped groups know that Rocky Mount is willing to accommodate them, it has been able, without additional expense or trouble, to adapt its regular program to their special needs.

VII. An Outreach Program for Nursing-Home Residents

The Oswego County Historical Society, Oswego, New York, is a non-profit organization founded in 1896, with a membership of 450. The society owns the Richardson-Bates House Museum, a large Italianate villa complete with its original nineteenth-century furnishings. The society's programs include a permanent exhibition about the history of the county, four changing exhibitions per year, public lectures, a journal, a research library, and permanent collections of artifacts concerning county history. An educational outreach program serves schools, nursing homes, and other organizations requesting information on county history.

In 1979, the Oswego County Historical Society's director of education made nineteen presentations in six different nursing homes and housing units for the elderly. She used genuine museum artifacts from our collection to illustrate these talks. Topics included crafts such as spinning, weaving, and quilting, rural living in nineteenth-century Oswego County, folklore of Oswego County, the county's role in the Civil War, and architecture of Oswego County.

Recently, at a local nursing home, the education director led a series of discussions entitled "Exploring Local History." The teaching materials were secured from the National Council on the Aging, through the support of the National Endowment for the Humanities, a federal agency. This program was so successful that a second series, "The Remembered Past, 1914–1945," will be taught this spring. In the meantime, the education director will begin a training program for volunteer discussion leaders, who will be available to organize these programs throughout the county.

It has been our experience that nursing-home patients like to handle objects, since their acuity of sight and hearing are not integral to their enjoyment of the objects. Objects differ in size, texture, odor, and weight, and we invite attendants to help pass them around so that each person can have an opportunity to feel and smell. Everyone has enjoyed this very much.

For Further Reading

Since most of the scant and widely-scattered literature on museum accessibility was written by professionals on the basis of their experience in large museums, it may give the staff members of small museums and historical organizations some ideas, but they should not jump to the conclusion that the process need be as time-consuming and expensive as some of these works imply. The fundamentally important publications of the National Information Center for Arts and the Handicapped (ARTS) include a worthwhile series of pamphlets describing programs at museums all over the country. They also give valuable practical suggestions and sources of further information; their bibliographies are particularly useful. They include "An Issue of Access," "Architectural Accessibility," and "Arts for the Blind and Visually Impaired People," "504 and the Visual Arts" is the most up-to-date explanation of how to comply with the NEA guidelines. All historical organizations should be on the mailing list for these free publications, which are available without charge from the Arts and Special Constituencies Program, National Endowment for the Arts, 2401 E Street N.W., Washington, D.C. 20506.

At present, the leading authority on museum accessibility is Larry Molloy, Director of ARTS. His publications include "504 Regulations: Learning to Live by the Rules," *Museum News* (September-October 1978), which gives valuable background on the origin and meaning of the Rehabilitation Act of 1973. "One Way to Comply with Section 504," *Museum News* (March-April 1979), discusses the steps to compliance in terms that may be more useful to large museums than to small historical societies. Alice P. Kenney has concentrated primarily on the small museum in "Museums from a Wheelchair," *Museum News* (December 1974) and "A Test of Barrier-Free Design," *Museum News* (January-February 1977), which describes a wheelchair tour of a local art museum. "Open Door for the Handicapped," *Historic Preservation* (June-September 1978) explains efforts being made to overcome obstacles at the historic house museums of the National Trust for Historic Preservation. *Hospitable Heritage: The Report of MUSEUM ACCESS* (Allentown, Pa.: Lehigh County Historical Society, 1979) tells about a survey of accessibility at small museums in southeastern Pennsylvania.

Even small historical societies will want to be familiar with basic directories and bibliographies, which should be available in the local or regional public library. *Selected Federal Publications Concerning the Handicapped* (Department of Health, Education, and Welfare, Office of Handicapped Individuals, Washington, D.C.) is a guide to publications available from

HEW and other government agencies on a number of subjects, of which those of most interest to historical organizations are architectural barriers, legislation, education, and travel. The world of disability is introduced in *Directory of Organizations Interested in the Handicapped* (Committee for the Handicapped, People to People Program, Washington, D.C.) and *Directory of National Information Services and Handicapping Conditions and Related Services* (Clearinghouse on the Handicapped, Office of Handicapped Individuals, Washington, D.C.). Sources of federal funds are listed in *Federal Assistance for Programs Serving the Handicapped* (Clearinghouse for the Handicapped, Office of Handicapped Individuals, Washington, D.C.). Burton J. Eckstein, editor, *Handicapped Funding Directory: A Research Grant Guide* (Oceanside, N.Y., 1978) gives an overview of both public and private funding organizations and some useful suggestions for writing proposals. Directories of local agencies serving the handicapped may be secured from state and local human resources offices.

Most of the literature on architectural accessibility is written for architects and is extremely technical, but historical organization staff members may wish to consult it to see what is involved. One exception is a pamphlet prepared to acquaint the general public with the meaning of the Architectural Barriers Act of 1968, its machinery for enforcement, and procedures for complaints by the Architectural and Transportation Barriers Compliance Board, *Access America: The Architectural Barriers Act and You* (Washington, D.C.). The same board published a massive *Resource Guide to Literature on Barrier-Free Environments with Selected Annotations* (Washington, D.C., 1977), which includes comprehensive sections on architecture in parks and historic sites as well as many other subjects. The official statement of ANSI standards for all disabilities is *American National Standards Institute Specifications for Making Buildings Accessible to and Usable by the Handicapped* (New York: American National Standards Institute, 1961). Graphic representations of one state's building code requirements for ramps, elevators, and washrooms may be found in Ronald L. Mace, *Illustrated Handbook of the Handicapped Section of the North Carolina State Building Code* (Raleigh, N.C.: North Carolina Department of Insurance, Special Office of the Handicapped, 1974), *Addenda to the Illustrated Handbook . . .* (Raleigh, N.C., 1975). His *Accessibility Modifications: Guidelines for Modification of Existing Buildings for Accessibility to the Handicapped* (Raleigh, N.C., 1976) concerns primarily institutions and public buildings, but the principles discussed are applicable to all buildings. Two helpful items published by the National Research Council of Canada are D. N. Henning, *Annotated Bibliography on Building for Disabled Persons* (Ottawa, Canada: National Research Council, Division of Building Research, 1971) and *Checklist for Building Use by the Handicapped* (Ottawa, Canada: National Research Council, Division of Building Research, 1971), which contains a section on museums and exhibition buildings.

A number of useful bibliographies of materials concerning the blind are distributed by the M.C. Migel Memorial Library (American Foundation for the Blind, New York, N.Y.), which will lend particular items mentioned in them if they are not otherwise available. Charles W. Stanford, Jr., "Art for Humanity's Sake" (North Carolina Museum of Art, 1976), tells the story of the pioneer Mary Duke Biddle tactile gallery, with sympathetic insights into what the blind learned and what the sighted learned from the blind, and valuable suggestions of what should be avoided in planning similar museums elsewhere. A similar experiment at the Lions Gallery of the Wadsworth Atheneum in Hartford, Conn., which at the insistence of the blind themselves was expanded to include all the senses and all visitors is described in Susan Gans, "Developing Museum Experiences for Handicapped Visitors" (*Concepts,* Hillsboro Museum, Tampa, Fla.). Nelson Coons, *The Place of the Museum in the Education of the Blind* (New York: American Foundation for the Blind, 1953) discusses the contributions of the museum of the Perkins Institute to that school's curriculum. Harry Hendrickson, "Your Museum: A Resource for the Blind") *Museum News,* October, 1971) tells about services provided to blind children as part of the total program of the University of Illinois Museum of Natural History. A Smithsonian Institution project to improve service to the blind, which also increased staff awareness of the needs of all handicapped visitors, is reported in Dove Toll, *Should Museums Serve the Visually Handicapped?* (September 1975).

An introduction to education projects for special populations is *Museums and Handicapped Students: Guidelines for Educators* (Washington, D.C.: Smithsonian Institution, 1977), which presents a practical discussion of the difficulties created by different disabilities, the most comprehensive treatment of that subject now available. Valuable works from the National Park Service include Freeman J. Tilden, *Interpreting Our Heritage* (Chapel Hill, N.C.: University of North Carolina Press, 1959), whose general principles may profitably be applied to handicapped visitors, and Jacques Beechel, *Interpretation for Handicapped Persons* (Seattle, Wash.: National Park Service, Pacific Northwest Conference, 1975), which gives more practical suggestions for communicating with persons with various disabilities. Cathy B. Callow, "Museums and the Disabled," *Museum Journal* (September 1974), surveys ways in which thirty-five museums serve visitors in wheelchairs. Virginia Cassiano, "Cultural Development of Handicapped Individuals" (Report to the White House Conference on the Handicapped) explores discrimination against handicapped artists and the importance to the handicapped of creative arts, art therapy, and art education. A very interesting outreach program is presented in *Trip-Out Trucks and Trunks* (DeYoung Museum School of Art, San Francisco). The trail-blazing Metropolitan Museum of Art project for museum experiences for retarded adults is discussed by Charles Steiner in "Reaching the Mentally Handicapped," *Museum News* (July-August 1978), *Museum Programs for Retarded Adults* and *Museums for the Disabled* (New York: Metropolitan Museum of Art, 1978, 1979).

Handicapped individuals, agencies that work with the handicapped, and the public library can direct the personnel of museums and historical organizations to a wide variety of literature about what it means to be a disabled individual. A few helpful items include *People in Wheelchairs: Hints for Helpers* (British Red Cross Society, London), which contains very practical suggestions for people pushing wheelchairs. Donna Bluhm, *Teaching the Retarded Visually Handicapped: Indeed They are Children* (Philadelphia: W. B. Saunders, 1968) introduces materials and curriculum methods used in this form of special education. *The Invisible Battle* and *Beyond the Sound Barrier* (Washington, D.C.: George Washington University Barrier Awareness Project, 1978) are pamphlets designed to enlighten the general public on attitudinal barriers that tend to isolate handicapped persons from the world around them. In "Uncle Tom and Tiny Tim," *American Scholar* (Summer 1969), Leonard Kriegel identifies the handicapped as a minority by perceptive comparison of the experience of disabled persons with that of early twentieth-century immigrants and present-day blacks. Important periodicals include *Accent on Living,* written by and for disabled persons, *Rehabilitation Gazette,* an international journal presenting the views of that profession, and the magazines of such organizations as the Paralyzed Veterans of America. The historical organization should also ask to be placed on the mailing list of local groups of handicapped persons.

Index

Accessibility: of historic structures, 14, 16–17, 36; publicizing, 18–19, 92–93; lack of funds as obstacle to, 19; "accessible" definition, 28, 48–49; and visits to museums, 29–30. *See also* American National Standards Institute; Structures

Accessibilty symbol, international, 29, 30, 57

Advance notice: for visits or tours, 33, 53, 80, 91, 115

Advance planning, 84–89

Advertising. *See* Media; Public relations

Advisory committee: membership, 18; organization, 38–39; and agencies, 38–39, 95; and the self-evaluation form, 39–40; disabled people as members, 10, 37, 42, 116–117; and the civil rights movement, 43; and the "transition plan," 48; and mechanical adaptation techniques, 58–59; at the Nebraska State Historical Society, 116–117

Agencies: consultation with, 37–38; and the advisory committee, 38–39; co-operation with historical societies, 83–84, 95; and fund-raising, 93

American Association for State and Local History, 11, 67, 90, 93

American Association of Museums, 93

American Federation of the Blind, 47

American National Standards Institute (ANSI), 49, 53–56 *passim*

Architectural Barriers Act of 1968, 23, 49

Auditoriums, 34, 65

Audio tapes, 65

Audiovisual interpretation: of buildings' second floor, 10–11, 86; captioned, 65; and outreach programs, 90

Barriers: wide range of, 3; inaccessible facilities and programs, 7; "barrier-free" definition, 28, 48–49; of structures, 29–30; removal of, at the Nebraska State Historical Society,

115–116. *See also* Stairs and steps; Walk surfaces

Bicentennial celebration: and historic heritage, 3, 96; commemorative volumes, 13; sign-language tours, 88; effects of, 99–100

Blindness: statistics, 4–5; tactile exhibits, 47, 58, 62–63; maps and models useful, 62; libraries for the blind, 63–64; advance planning for tours, 86. *See also* Radio reading stations; Touch; Visual impairments

Board of directors, 18, 24–25, 48

Boat: as historic property, 116

Braille, 58, 64, 117

Brochures: of societies, 13; use of large-type format for, 32, 64; taped, 63; emphasis on accessible features, 89–90; good qualities of, 90–91

Buildings. *See* Structures

Captions: for photographic slides, 65

Cassette recordings, 58, 59, 60, 63

CETA employees, 8, 16, 25

Chairs, 31. *See also* Wheelchairs

Children: "mainstreamed," 5, 35, 73, 75; as handicapped visitors, 7, 120; emotionally disturbed, 75. *See also* Dyslexia; Learning disabilities

Christmas party: for handicapped children, 89

Civil rights movement, 3, 9, 23, 43

Colonial Williamsburg, 99

Compliance officer: for organizations implementing Section 504, 18

Co-ordinator, 10, 27, 37–39, 48

Crafts, 14, 99, 120, 121

Crutches, 50, 53

Curb cuts, 30, 85

Deaf Awareness Week, 87

Deafness: statistics, 5; appropriate materials for, 65–66; deaf people think in pictures, 66, 88; effective communication with, 70–71, 91; sign-language tours, 87–88.

Deafness (*Cont.*) *See also* Hearing aids; Lip-reading; Sign language

Director, 15, 26, 50

Directors, board of, 18, 24–25, 48

Disability: the word and some definitions, 4, 78

Disabled people: and discrimination, 3; and employment, 4; statistics, 4; laws and ordinances prohibiting discrimination against, 8, 27; as members of advisory committee, 10, 37, 42, 116–117; as volunteers, 16, 98; insensitivity of the community to, 19; and programs of museums and historical organizations, 19, 29, 43, 47; adjustments necessary for employees, 26; sociological differences, 40–41; *disabled*, as a term, distinguished from *handicapped*, 78; and the impression of helplessness, 79; confusion about types of, 79–80; communication networks among, 92–93; as invaluable employees, 98; and contributions to historical organizations, 101. *See also* Children; Elderly people; Employment; Personnel; Volunteers

Discrimination: and disabled people, 3; and employment, 8, 18; laws and ordinances prohibiting, 8, 25–27; reverse, 77–78

Dogs, guide, 4, 69, 84

Doors: width for wheelchairs, 30; specifications for, 49; security, 116

Dyslexia, 5, 74

Elderly people: and disability, 4, 6; and historical societies, 6, 35–36; as volunteers, 16; and museum tours, 33, 50–51; as majority of the handicapped audience, 42; collecting the memories of, 98; outreach programs of the Oswego County Historical Society, 120–121

Electronic amplification, 17, 59, 64–65

Elevators, 23, 49, 55–56. *See also* Escalators; Lifts

Employment: question on 1980 census form, 4; and discrimination, 18, 25; and Section 504, 8, 25–26

Equipment, 66–67, 95, 118–119

Escalators, 54. *See also* Elevators; Lifts

Exhibits: behind glass, 31; traveling, 35–36; tactile, 47, 58, 62–63; for people with limited vision, 119

Films: as historical society programs, 13, 14; and accessible auditoriums, 34; captions for, 35; rented, 66; film strip valuable for interpretation at the Paul Revere House, 115

Financial support: federal assistance, 16, 17, 25; fund-raising, 89; co-operation with agencies, 93; for renovations, 93–94; private sources of, 95; funds difficult to secure, 97

Fire, 34

Floors, 31

Folk art, 100, 117, 119

Fulton County Historical Society (Rochester, Indiana), 119

Funds. *See* Financial support

Genealogy, 14, 100, 119

Gift shop, 31, 63

Gloves: and touch technique for museum holdings, 32, 33

Guide dogs, 4, 69, 84

Guides: *See* Personnel; Volunteers

Hallways, 49

Handicap: the word and some definitions, 78, 79

Handicapped people. *See* Children; Disabled people; Elderly people; Employment

Handrails, 54

Hands, 51

Hazards, 30, 34, 51–57 *passim*

Hearing aids, 5, 65

Hearing difficulties. *See* Deafness

HEW Office of Museum Services, 8, 16, 27, 94

Historic preservation: national awareness weeks, 92; and historical societies' programs, 13–14, 94; and outreach programs, 97–98; impetus from the bicentennial celebration, 99–100

Historic Preservation Act of 1966, 9

Historical societies (organizations): program accessibility, 9, 10, 27–28; characteristics of, 12; and walking tours, 12; and guided tours, 12, 13, 29; program activities of, 12, 29; publication programs, 13; libraries, 13, 14; historic preservation activities, 13–14, 94, 101; access problems, 14, 16–19, 49–50; policy statements, 24–25; "Needs Assessment Survey Instrument," 27; history and purpose presentation, 38;

Historical societies (*Cont.*)
and programs close to the intention of
Section 504, 47; co-operation with
agencies, 83–84, 95; hours of opening,
91; information on successful
program adaptations, 93; reason for
existence of, 95–96; responsibility to
entire community, 96; shifts in
emphasis of programs, 96–97;
reinforcement of important national
values, 100–101; functions of, 101.
See also Crafts; Financial support;
Museum villages; Oral history;
Outreach programs; Personnel;
Public relations; Structures;
Volunteers
History: and social studies emphasis,
90, 100–101
Hours of opening: at museums and
historic sites, 91
Hydraulic lift, 85. *See also* Lifts

International accessibility symbol, 29,
30, 57
Insurance, 69

Labels, 32, 64
Language, 70–71, 78–79, 90
Learning disabilities, 5, 73–75
Lehigh County Historical Society,
(Allentown, Pa.), 117–119
Libraries: of historical societies, 13, 14;
disabled users and access to, 33–34;
for the blind, 63–64. *See also* Radio
reading stations
Lifts, 53, 56, 85. *See also* Elevators;
Escalators
Lions Gallery of the Senses (Wadsworth
Atheneum, Connecticut), 47
Lip-reading, 5, 71. *See also* Deafness

Macon County Museum Complex
(Decatur, Ill.), 117
Magnification process, 64
Magnifying glass, 70
Maps, 58, 62
Markers, 36–37. *See also* Signs
Mary Duke Biddle Gallery (North
Carolina Museum of Art), 47
Media, 29, 84, 90, 92–93. *See also* Films;
Radio reading stations; Television;
Videotape
Mental illness, 5, 40, 73
Mental retardation, 17, 75–77, 84,
88–89
Metropolitan Museum of Art, 88–89

Minorities, 94
Mobility, limited, 4, 10, 29, 40
Models, 58, 62
Museum holdings. *See* Objects
Museum, mobile, 116
Museum villages; wide variety of, 14;
problem of distance and uneven walk
surfaces, 49–50, 57–58; use of small
vehicles, 58; Prairie Village at the
Macon County Museum Complex, 117

National Advisory Council on Historic
Preservation, 9, 106
National Council on the Aging, 121
National Endowment for the Arts: and
Section 504, 8, 9, 105; source of
grants, 16, 94; Art and Special
Constituencies Program of, 27;
literature available from, 27
National Endowment for the
Humanities, 16, 27, 94, 121
National Information Service for Arts
and the Handicapped (ARTS), 27, 93
National Register of Historic Places, 9,
14, 106
National Science Foundation, 16, 27, 94
National Trust for Historic
Preservation, 3, 36, 49, 93
Nebraska State Historical Society,
115–117
"Needs Assessment Survey
Instrument," 27
Newsletters, 13, 92
Nursing homes, 11, 13, 35, 120–121

Objects: exhibits of, 5, 47, 59, 62–63;
analogies in describing, 70; touching,
85, 87, 121. *See also* Touch
Obstacles. *See* Barriers; Hazards
Office of Museum Services. *See* HEW
Office of Museum Services
Old age. *See* Elderly people
Oral history, 11, 14, 36
Oswego County Historical Society
(Oswego, N.Y.), 120–121
Outreach programs: for elderly people,
6, 11, 13, 35–36; development of,
35–36, 49, 90; and the process of
historic preservation, 97–98; of the
Oswego County Historical Society,
120–121

Parking, 29–30, 85
Paul Revere House (Boston, Mass.),
114–115
Perkins Institute (Boston, Mass.), 47

Personnel: staff of historical societies, 14–16; insufficient, 19; and disabled employees, 26, 98; need training to assist disabled persons, 29; training in use of equipment, 66–67; meetings on types of disabilities, 67–69; attitudes of, 77–80; advance planning for visitors, 84–89; staff guidelines, 86; need complete information, 91; their reason for being, 96; staff training at the Paul Revere House, 115. *See also* Volunteers
Policy statement, 24–25
Prairie Village, 117
Public relations, 18–19, 25, 29, 90–93 *passim*. *See also* Media; Talk shows

Radio reading stations: and local history materials, 11, 17, 64; and publicity, 29, 58, 92–93. *See also* Libraries
Ramps: replacing steps, 23, 51, 53; specifications for, 49; at the Nebraska State Historical Society, 116; at the Macon County Museum Complex, 117; at the Lehigh County Historical Society, 117–118
Recordings. *See* Cassette recordings
Rehabilitation Act of 1973 (P.L. 93–112, 1973), 3, 8, 23, 43, 105. *See also* Section 504
Retardation. *See* Mental retardation
Rest rooms, 49, 56–57
Revenue sharing, 8, 16–18 *passim*, 25
Rocky Mount Historical Association (Tennessee), 120
Rugs, 31
Runners, 31

Safety regulations, 34
Second floor (of historic buildings): audiovisual interpretation of, 10, 58–60, 86; at the Paul Revere House, 114–115; videotape interpretation of, 117–119
Section 504: compliance with, 3, 17–18, 24–25; guidelines for, 7–10, 27, 37, 105–106; "transition plan," 8–9, 10, 18, 48; and self-evaluation, 10, 18, 39–40; and employment practices, 25–26; integration of disabled persons into existing programs, 19, 29, 43, 47; and tactile exhibits, 47; and persons with mental illness, 73; fund-raising for renovations, 93–94. *See also*

Rehabilitation Act of 1973 (P.L. 93–112, 1973)
Self-evaluation, 10, 18, 39–40
Senior citizens' centers, 11, 13, 18, 20
Sign-language: use by the deaf, 5, 71–72; and tours for deaf groups, 19–20, 43, 87–88; interpreters, 17, 34–35, 59; on videotape, 72. *See also* Deafness; Lip-reading
Signs, 29
Site marking, 36–37
Slides, 14, 59–61, 65, 119
Social studies, 90, 100
Staff. *See* Personnel; Volunteers
Stairs and steps: hazards, 6, 54–56 *passim*; and entrances, 30, 51, 53; specifications for, 49, 53–54; stair lifts, 53, 56; at the Paul Revere House, 114
State agencies. *See* Agencies
Steamer, 116
Steps. *See* Stairs and steps
Structures: historic, integrity of, 3, 23, 36; "buildings are preserved for people," 3, 36; transition plan for modifications, 8–9, 10, 18, 48; access problems, 14, 16–19, 49–50; and entrances, 30, 51, 53, 85–86; compliance with building codes, 48; funding for alterations, 94. *See also* Accessibility; Barriers; Second floor

Talk shows, 92, 93
Telephones, public, 32, 49
Television, 38, 72, 90, 92, 119. *See also* Talk shows; Videotape
"Thermoform," 64
Toilets. *See* Rest rooms
Touch: of objects, 5, 17, 59, 63; privileges of, 32–33; tactile exhibits, 47, 58, 62–63; and blind visitors, 69–70; and visitors with learning disabilities, 74. *See also* Blindness
Trailer, 58, 116
Transition plan. *See under* Section 504; Structures
Transportation: and disability, 4; inadequate, 7; limitations of, 83; advance arrangement for, 91
Typewriter, large-type, 32, 66

U.S. Department of Health, Education, and Welfare. *See* HEW Office of Museum Services; Section 504

U.S. Department of the Interior, 9, 49, 105–106

U.S. National Park Service, 9, 50

Vehicles, 58, 92, 116

Videotape: documenting crafts, 14; for television, 38, 61–62; and equipment, 66; and sign-language interpretations, 72; prepared by the Lehigh County Historical Society, 117–119. *See also* Television

Visual impairment: and colors, 5, 86, 90; programs and facilities, 11; rules for exhibits for, 119. *See also* Blindness

Volunteers: and historical societies, 6, 15–16; training of, 29, 66, 67; meetings on types of disabilities, 67–69; advance planning for visitors, 84–89; disabled people as, 98. *See also* Personnel

Waivers, 9, 49, 69

Walk surfaces, 6, 30, 49, 51, 57–58

Walker with a seat, 92

Water fountains, 32, 49

Wheelchairs: accommodation of, 29, 30; clamp-on mirrors for 31; and safety regulations, 34; needs of visitors, 50 51, 53; experience for personnel, 68; implications of being confined to, 79; tours by persons in, 85–86; used with delight, 92; accessibility for people at the Paul Revere House, 114

Words. *See* Language